YOU CAN

MAKE A

DIFFERENCE

OTHER BOOKS BY ANTHONY CAMPOLO

Carpe Diem

Following Jesus Without Embarrassing God

20 Hot Potatoes Christians Are Afraid to Touch

It's Friday, but Sunday's Comin'

Let Me Tell You a Story

Which Jesus?

TONY CAMPOLO

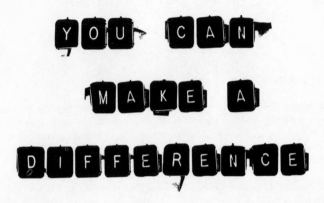

YOU CAN MAKE A DIFFERENCE

HIGH-VOLTAGE LIVING IN A BURNED-OUT WORLD

W PUBLISHING GROUP™

www.wpublishinggroup.com

A Division of Thomas Nelson, Inc.
www.ThomasNelson.com

To my big sisters
Rose and Ann
who taught me how to have fun

YOU CAN MAKE A DIFFERENCE

Published by W Publishing Group, a Division of Thomas Nelson, Inc., P.O. Box 141000, Nashville, TN, 37214.

Unless otherwise indicated, Scripture quotations used in this book are from the King James Version of the Bible (KJV). Other Scripture references are from the following source:

The Holy Bible, New International Version (NIV) © 1973, 1978, 1984, International Bible Society. Used by permission of Zondervan Bible Publishers.

Library of Congress Cataloging-in-Publication Data

Campolo, Anthony
    You can make a difference.
    ISBN 0-8499-1784-0 (hardcover)
    1. Youth—Religious Life. 2. Campolo, Anthony. [I. Christian Life] I. Title
    BV4531.2.C315   1984
    248.8'3
                                                        83-26024

Printed in the United States of America
03 04 05 06 07 BVG 9 8 7 6 5 4 3

CONTENTS

INTRODUCTION

YOU CAN MAKE A DIFFERENCE

A lot of young people become believers in Christ without becoming disciples. That means that they do not measure up to the high calling that God has for them. This book describes what is involved in discipleship. In it, I attempt to spell out the steps that must be taken if the young Christian is to become a true follower of Jesus Christ.

Making it into adulthood as a mature Christian is a difficult task. There are so many forces at work to get a young Christian off track. The consumerism that impacts the consciousness through the media, the sexual temptations that seem omnipresent, the pressure of parents to aspire to the success values of the dominant culture, and the confusion that seems to overwhelm young people in the face of the multiple decisions they have to make can all conspire to psychologically wear out any Christian trying to become a true disciple.

In speaking to young people from one end of America to the other, as well as in countries like Australia, New Zealand, South Africa, and the United Kingdom, I find that there are certain common issues that need to be addressed. Young people recognize that, if they don't handle their dating life right, they can end up in lifelong relationships that will suppress their desires for becoming all that God wants them to be. They are looking for some direction on how to date and how to develop solid, loving relationships.

In this book, I do my best to spell out the steps for maintaining a good devotional life. I emphasize the necessity for every young Christian to develop a small group with two or three others of like mind and heart who can provide support and encouragement in the Christian journey. I am a sociologist. Those of us in the field refer to such small groups as "plausibility structures." What that means is that Christ will stay real in the consciousness, and the individual will stay faithful to convictions primarily as a result of having regular get-togethers with like-minded persons who hold them accountable for living the consistent Christian life. These support groups help young believers find the strength to stand up against those forces in the youth culture that can easily annihilate the faith of those who would be Christians.

A good part of this book is dedicated to helping young people find their mission in life. Being a Christian isn't just believing in God and being good. It involves a commitment to change the world. Christians are expected to be part of a movement that will make the world that is, into the world that ought to be. All of us are expected to witness for Christ in what we say and do in everyday life. But beyond that, it is important that each young person be constantly striving to figure out the best way his or her talents and abilities can be used to impact the world for the good that God wants to accomplish.

In today's society, many young people grow cynical and don't believe that they can account for much. Everywhere I go I meet high-school and university students who shrug their shoulders in the face of the awesome challenges of our world and say that they do not think they can make a difference. This book is designed to make a contrary case. By the grace of God, each person can make a difference. God created us to be world changers and I hope this book specifically helps you to define what that means for your life.

Tony Campolo
Eastern University
St. Davids, PA

COMMITMENT

GETTING BEYOND GOOD INTENTIONS

I teach at a small, church-related school near Philadelphia called Eastern College. Every May students come into my office, sit down, look at me across the desk, and say something like this: "Doc, I'm not coming back next semester."

I whip off my glasses, peer nearsightedly at them, and try to look professional. "Pray tell," I say. "Why?" They always look back at me with a strained look and say, "I need time, Doc, I need time." I say to myself, "This guy's done nothing for the past six months—and now he needs time?"

I know what he is going to say next. He's going to say, "I need time to find myself." There is a whole generation out there trying to find themselves, and they all look in the same place: Boulder, Colorado.

Then it gets real strange in a hurry. The kid says, "Doc, Doc, I'm tired of playing all these roles that society says I have to play. I'm tired of being the me that my friends expect me to be, the me that the church expects me to be, the me that my parents expect me to be. I've got to peel away each of these socially prescribed identities. I've got to peel away each of these socially constructed roles. I've got to peel them away—do you hear?—and come to grips with the core of my being, the essence of my personality!"

To all of this I have a simple retort: "Fella, suppose after you peel away each of these socially prescribed identities, after you peel away each of these socially created selves, you discover you are an onion! Now, *that* is a *real* possibility. You peel away all of the skins of the onion, what's left? Nothing. The onion is nothing more than the sum total of its skins."

It just may be that the human personality is nothing more than the sum total of all the roles society has trained him or her to play. That is, after he/she peels away each of these socially generated selves and takes the long journey into his/her inner self, and gets there, he or she will discover "Hi-ho, nobody's home!" Now that's a real possibility.

You see, there is a common presupposition that everybody has a "self" waiting to be found. I don't believe that. I don't believe that there is an essential self waiting to be found through introspection. If there were, somebody would have found it long ago. Of the thousands of young people who have taken time off to find themselves, you would think that somebody would eventually come back and say, "Doc! Doc, I found myself just north of Cleveland!" But it never happens.

That's because there is no such thing as a self waiting to be found. Quite to the contrary, the self is something waiting to be created. And there is only one way to create a self; there is only one way to create an identity; there is only one way to create meaning in life; and that, friends, is through commitment. Only through commitment do people achieve an identity and a meaning and a purpose in life. And there are very few committed people in this world.

As a matter of fact, one of the few places I see committed people is in airports. That's funny, you say, committed people in the airports? Of course I'm referring to the Hare Krishna people. I like them, but they are strange! I fly in and out of the Philadelphia airport a lot and I've gotten to know some of the ones who hang out there. Since I know them, I usually can get to them before they get to me. I usually sneak up on their blind side, grab them, spin them around, kiss them on the cheek, and say, "Jesus loves you!" It blows them away. I don't win many converts that way, but it's lots of fun. However, there's one thing I have to say about the followers of Hare Krishna: they are committed people. Consequently, they are people who have an identity, a clear definition of selfhood, and a well-established meaning to life. Their only problem is that their god isn't real and they are deceived.

Today you are being called to commit your life to Jesus Christ. He *is* real. He's every bit as real as you are. He is with you this very moment. He wants you to establish your identity in Him. He wants you to create your purpose for life in service to His cause. He calls you to define who you are by understanding what He has called you to become. You are determined by your commitment, and you *are* a Christian if you have committed your life to Jesus.

One of my favorite stories describing commitment is about a tightrope walker named Blondin. In the late 1890s he strung a tightrope across Niagara Falls, and then before ten thousand screaming people, inched his way from the Canadian side of the falls to the U.S. side. When he got there, the crowd began shouting his name, "Blondin! Blondin! Blondin! Blondin!"

Finally he raised his arms, quieted the crowd, and (how's this for an ego trip?) shouted to them, "I am Blondin! Do you believe in me?" The crowd shouted back, "We believe! We believe! We believe!"

Again he quieted the crowd and once more he shouted to them, "I'm going back across the tightrope, but this time I'm going to carry someone on my back. Do you believe I can do that?" The crowd yelled, "We believe! We believe!"

He quieted them one more time and then he said, "Who will be that person?" The crowd went dead. Nothing.

Finally, out of the crowd stepped one man. He climbed on Blondin's shoulders and for the next three and a half hours, Blondin inched his way back across the tightrope to the Canadian side of the falls.

The point of the story is blatantly clear: ten thousand people stood there that day chanting, "We believe, we believe!" but only one person really believed. Believing is not just saying, "I accept the facts." Believing is giving your life over into the hands of the one in whom you say you believe. Believing is a commitment.

The most serious problem with the church today is that while it is filled with believers, it is seriously devoid of committed disciples. Oh, everybody believes. Everywhere I go, I find believers. As I travel from one end of this country to the other, I find that we are a nation with almost a hundred million people who call themselves "born again." But I wonder how many of them are committed. I wonder what Jesus really means to them.

You could go down to a local bar and nudge the guy next to you and ask, "Do you believe in Jesus?" In all probability, he would say that he does believe in Jesus. He may be half bombed as he sits at the bar, but he still believes in Jesus. If you asked him theological questions, his answers would probably sound as evangelical as any you have ever heard. But that does not make him a Christian. That's because the thing that makes a person a Christian is not believing the right stuff, but whether or not that person is committed to Jesus. Being a Christian is dependent upon a person's turning over his or her life to Jesus so that Jesus can use that person to do the things He wants to do in this world. A person is a Christian when he or she becomes totally committed to changing the things that God wants changed.

Are you committed? That's the big question. Are you willing to do whatever Jesus wants you to do? Are you willing to be whatever Jesus wants you to be? Are you willing to go wherever Jesus wants you to go? Jesus offers no "cheap grace." He does not call you to be a nice believer. He calls you to committed discipleship.

When I was a kid, I read a book by an author named Sheldon. The book is called *In His Steps*. It has a simple premise: to be a Christian is to *commit* yourself to do whatever Jesus would do if He were in your shoes; to act as Jesus would act if He were in your place; to make the decisions Jesus would make if He were faced with your options. The book moved me as I read it, and I decided to commit myself to Christ as Sheldon suggested. I decided to do whatever Jesus would do if Jesus were in my shoes. That was going to be my thing from that moment on. Whatever He'd do, I'd do. I was committed.

The day after making that decision, I went to my high school, West Philadelphia High. It was a great school, and I was in the neatest homeroom in the place, Homeroom 48! Homeroom 48 was where the jocks were assigned. And I was a jock. Now I want you to know that being a jock is more than simply being an athlete. Athletes may play sports, but jocks have style. You can always tell a real jock. A jock doesn't just walk, a jock *moves*. You have to be cool to be a jock. A jock is the kind of guy who *moves* down the hallways at school and expects the girls to line up along the walls and sing "How Great Thou Art."

All the jocks were in Homeroom 48. The football players, the basketball players, the wrestlers. But in addition to the jocks and superstars, there were also four kids who didn't belong. They were the members of the chess team. Now don't get me wrong—not all chess players are like these guys, but the chess team at West Philadelphia High that year was made up of "wimps." If that word doesn't communicate, let's try "nerds." You know the kind of kids I'm talking about. I'm describing the kind of kid who, on a rainy day, comes to school wearing *galoshes*. Or brings his lunch in a brown paper bag—and saves the bag!

As I coolly *moved* into my homeroom, an urgent but simple question came to me: "If Jesus were in my place, who would He choose for a friend?" Would He sit with the superstars and the jocks? Would He choose to be with the "in" kids? Would He choose to identify with the popular kids? Or would Jesus go over and become a friend of the "wimps"?

It didn't take me long to resolve that line of questioning. Having read the Scriptures and learned about Jesus, I knew exactly what He would do. Jesus would have been a friend of the friendless. He would have sat with some wimp. I decided to do what He would do, so I went over and sat next to one. Strangely enough, we became friends and we stayed friends that entire year, right up until graduation.

Now I really wish this story had one of those storybook endings. I wish I could tell you, "Because I *loved* that wimp, because I *gave* myself to that wimp, because *I cared* for that wimp, that wimp *blossomed*! He became a *wholesome, powerful, dynamic* personality. And *today*, my friends, that wimp is *George Bush!*" I really wish this story had one of those Paul Harvey endings. Actually, in this particular case, the wimp stayed a wimp. As a matter of fact, I saw him in New York a year ago and he's still a wimp.

Religious stories don't always turn out to have glorious and wonderful endings. If you are going to follow Jesus, you do the things that Jesus would do without being concerned about how everything will turn out. You learn that there is joy in being faithful to what He requires of you, regardless of the results.

Doing what Jesus would do is at the very core of the Christian lifestyle. To be a follower of Christ means asking yourself every moment of every day, "How would Jesus act if He were in my shoes in my situation?" To be a Christian is to live out life as Jesus would live it regardless of how tough such a commitment proves to be.

When you start trying to be what Jesus would be, when you start trying to do what Jesus would do, you are going to discover that you are committed to a lifestyle that is tougher than anything else you've ever tried to do. Living the Christian life is incredibly difficult. In fact, when you try to imitate Jesus for any length of time, you'll discover that you don't have what it takes. You will find that in your attempt to do what Jesus would do if He were in your shoes, you will fail over and over again.

In my early days as a Christian, I failed day after day after day. I'd say, "God, I did these things wrong," and I would list all the ways I'd failed to do what Jesus would do and be what Jesus would be. Then I'd add, "Lord, tomorrow I'm going to do better."

Then I'd go out the next day and usually do exactly those things that I had told God I wouldn't do the night before. And at the end of the day I'd get down and confess my shortcomings again. But I would fail over and over again. It would go on and on like that. It got to the point where I just felt like praying "ditto" each night.

In more recent years, I have learned the reason for my continual failures. I have learned that there's a big difference between my trying to live for Jesus and allowing Jesus to live through me. Let me put it another way. There's a big difference between my trying to do something for Him and His trying to do something *through* me. Got that?

You see, what Jesus wants to do is to come into my life and into your life and help us to live out His will. He doesn't simply ask us to do what He would do! He offers to come in and possess us so that He can enable us to do what we could never do ourselves. This is a crucial fact to remember. If each of us allows God to possess us and strengthen us, He will give to each of us the ability to do His will. Without Him, neither you nor I can live the life He wants us to live.

When I was a jock in high school, I ran track. I wasn't great, but I was okay. One day my coach took the whole track team to Franklin Field in Philadelphia to see the great Roger Bannister run a race. He was the first man to run the mile in less than four minutes, and we were all anxious to see if he could do it again.

Our entire team was standing and cheering as the world's greatest runners readied themselves for the final event of the meet, the mile run. I can remember the excitement as the race got under way. All the runners remained bunched for the first three laps. Then on the last lap, Bannister pulled away from the pack. The crowd went crazy as he picked up the pace and distanced himself from the other runners. Everyone in the stands knew he was going to do it again. The four-minute-mile barrier was about to be shattered again. When he crossed the finish line, the crowd exploded. People were screaming and jumping up and down. We all went bananas when they announced that Bannister had run another sub-four-minute mile.

But while we were all cheering, I happened to look down. I saw Roger Bannister collapse in exhaustion. After crossing the finish line he just passed out. A first-aid team hurried onto the field with a stretcher. They loaded Bannister on it and quickly carried him off the field.

And as they were carrying a "half-dead" Roger Bannister to the emergency room, my coach put his hand on my shoulder and said, "Tony, you're our miler. I expect you to do that." At that moment, as I saw Bannister's exhausted form disappear under the stands, two things went through my mind. Number one, I didn't know whether I ever *could* do that. I liked to run and I was a jock, but to be a great miler, to run the mile in less than four minutes, that was something else again. No way could I do it. I lacked the ability, I lacked the build (check out the picture of me on the flap—does that look like the face of a lean and hungry miler?).

Second, in addition to lacking the physical ability, I also lacked the will. I would have liked to have been a great runner, but not badly enough to risk dropping dead for old West Philly High.

It's the same with living like Jesus. Like you, I lack both the ability and the will to carry it off. There is an absence of the will power necessary to stick with our commitments to Christ. Second, there is an inability to do in our own strength what we know God wants us to do.

But here's the good news of the gospel: when you and I allow Jesus to come in and possess us, He enables us to will what neither of us could ever will before—He enables us to do what neither of us could ever do before. The Scripture says, "For it is God which worketh in you both to *will* and to *do* of his good pleasure" (Phil. 2:13).

What I want you to get is this. First, you must become committed to Jesus, and not just simply believe in Him. You must commit yourself to Him and say, "Jesus I'm Yours. I'm going to do whatever You want me to. I'm going to live the way You want me to live every moment of every day. I will try to imitate what You would do if You were in my shoes." Second, you must say to Jesus, "I want You to come into my life and possess me and enable me to do what I could never do on my own; to will what I could never will before; to live as I could never live in my own strength."

Here's some more good news: when that happens, when Jesus comes in and possesses you, you are going to know joy. In fact, you are going to know joy as you've never, ever known joy before. It will undoubtedly blow you away.

When Jesus takes total possession of you—when you are surrendered to Him—your life is marked by a spontaneous joy that makes you into a fun person. My son and daughter often say to me, "Dad, you are a nice guy but you are dangerous." I can appreciate that, and even agree with it. I know that the Spirit of God has created in me an aliveness that is hard to contain.

For instance, I become dangerous on elevators. Society has trained us to behave in certain ways when we get on elevators, particularly crowded elevators. If you get on a crowded elevator you are supposed to turn and face the door. However, I have discovered that there is a great deal of fun in just getting on a crowded elevator and not turning. Face to face with the other people, I like to say, "You are probably wondering why I called this meeting, aren't you?" That usually blows them away.

Near our home in Philadelphia there is a toll bridge that crosses the Delaware River. The toll on the bridge is twenty-five cents, but sometimes when I cross the bridge I give the toll-taker two quarters and I tell him, "One quarter is for me and the other is for my good friend who is in the car right behind me." I don't know who is in the car behind me, but I want to tell you that it is worth twenty-five cents just to pull away from the toll booth, look in the rearview mirror, and watch the toll-taker trying to explain it to the guy in the next car.

Whenever I talk about these things, people ask what it's got to do with being a Christian, and I must respond to such a question by saying, "Everything!" Being possessed by Jesus creates a spontaneity and a joy that send you bursting forth on the world as a fun person. That is why I tell you that as young people, giving your life to Christ will prove to be the best move you could possibly make. It doesn't curtail your joy and spontaneity. Instead, in your surrender to Christ you will find yourself possessed with a spirit of life that will make you a joy to everyone who knows you.

You know, that's not bad theology. I believe that God is a God of laughter, a God of fun, a God of joy. I want to make this next point very, very clear: if I didn't believe that your life would be overwhelmingly filled with joy in surrendering to Jesus, I wouldn't invite you to do it. I would not ask you to surrender your life to Jesus unless I was convinced that you would be filled with joy in a way that you cannot possibly imagine right now. The presence of Jesus in your life—the result of being totally committed to Him and His will—will make you into a person who knows joy, joy, joy; unspeakable joy.

There's a Pentecostal College near Eastern College where I teach. I'm not Pentecostal, but I talk so fast that I think they think I'm speaking in tongues, so it works out okay. One day they invited me to speak at a chapel service. I like speaking there because they are dynamic, happy people and I enjoy being with them.

Just before I spoke, eight guys took me into a back room of the chapel and got me down on my knees. Then they laid their hands on my head and prayed for me. That was good. I need all the prayer I can get.

There was only one problem. Those guys prayed a long time. And that's usually okay too. But the longer they prayed, the more tired they got. And the more tired they got, the more they leaned on my head. I want to tell you that when eight guys are leaning on your head, it doesn't feel so good.

One guy wasn't even praying for me. Instead he went on and on, praying for somebody named Charlie Stoltzfus. "Dear Lord," he shouted, "You know Charles Stoltzfus. He lives in that silver trailer down the road about a mile. You know the trailer, Lord, just down the road on the right-hand side." I felt like saying, "Knock it off, fella, what do you think God's doing? Saying, 'What's the address again?'"

Anyway, he went on and on and on: "Lord, Charlie told me this morning that he's decided to leave his wife and three kids. He told me that he was walking out on his family. Lord, step in, do something, bring the people in that family back together again!"

All the while, I'm kneeling there with eight guys leaning on my head and I'm asking myself, "When's this guy going to knock it off so I can get these Pentecostal preachers off my head?" But he kept going on and on about Charlie Stoltzfus's leaving his wife and kids, giving God constant reminders that he lived in a silver trailer a mile down the road on the right-hand side.

Finally, the prayers were over and I went into the pulpit and preached. After I was finished, I got in my car, drove to the Pennsylvania Turnpike, and headed for home.

As I drove onto the turnpike, I noticed a hitchhiker. Now, I know you're not supposed to pick them up, but I'm a preacher and whenever I can get anybody locked in as a captive audience, I do it. So I stopped and picked him up. We drove a few minutes and I said, "Hi, my name's Tony Campolo. What's your name?" He said, "My name is Charlie Stoltzfus." I couldn't believe it!

I got off the turnpike at the next exit and headed back. He got a bit uneasy with that and after a few minutes he said, "Hey, mister, where are you taking me?" I said, "I'm taking you *home*." He narrowed his eyes and asked, "Why?"

I said, "Because you just left your wife and three children, right?" That blew him away. "Yeah! Yeah, that's right." With shock written all over his face, he plastered himself against the car door and never took his eyes off me.

I drove off the turnpike at the next exit. Then I really did him in as I drove right to his silver trailer. When I pulled up, his eyes seemed to bulge as he asked, "How did you know that I lived here?" I said, "*God told me.*" (I believe God *did* tell me.)

We got out of the car and I ordered him to get in that trailer. Half shaking he answered, "Right, mister, sure! Sure! I'm going."

When he opened the trailer door his wife exclaimed,

"You're back! You're back!" He whispered in her ear and the more he talked, the bigger her eyes got.

Then I said with real authority, "The two of you sit down. I'm going to talk and you two are going to listen!" Man! Did they listen!

That afternoon I led those two young people to Jesus Christ. And today, that guy is a preacher of the gospel out in California.

You're thinking, "Hey, is being surrendered to Jesus all that wonderful? Is it all that filled with joy?" Please understand this: there is no greater joy than the joy that comes when you sense your life under the control of the Spirit of God. Then you know you are going to be used to do fantastic and wonderful things for God. There's nothing in the world like the joy that comes in being committed to Jesus and being possessed by Him—so that through you He can begin to do the things He would do if He were physically present on the earth in your shoes.

There's a lot of joy to the Christian life. But I don't want you to get the idea that it's all joy. There's also sorrow and suffering in following Jesus. The apostle Paul once prayed, ". . . that I may know him, and the power of his resurrection, and the fellowship of his sufferings" (Phil. 3:10). Most of us are willing to buy into the joyful experiences when we are possessed by His power, but we have to understand that there is no ecstasy unless we are willing to also experience His agony.

When you become a Christian and when Jesus Christ possesses you, one of the results will be that your heart will be broken by the things that break the heart of Jesus. The things that make Jesus cry will make you cry.

At Eastern College where I teach, I head up the sociology department. Each January we take students to the Dominican Republic and Haiti. I want my students to visit those places because I want them to see what Jesus sees. I want them to feel what Jesus feels. I want their hearts to be broken by the things that break Jesus' heart.

I remember one time when we were in Port-au-Prince, the capital city of Haiti, a little boy came crawling toward me on the sidewalk. He was crippled, not because he had been born crippled, but because as an infant his parents deliberately broke his arms and legs and made him into a cripple. His parents figured that a crippled child could collect more money begging from tourists than a child who was whole.

I grant you that this boy was an unusual case. But what happened to him was an expression of the cruelty that accompanies extreme poverty. It is an example of the things that break the heart of Jesus.

Some of my students and colleagues at Eastern College got together and started a feeding program in the city of Cap-Haitien, Haiti. We were trying to raise enough money to pay for feeding the many suffering children of that miserable city.

At first, we were able to feed only five hundred children. There were hundreds more in that city who were malnourished. There were tens of thousands in Haiti who were close to death. You know the job I wanted my college students to do down there? I didn't want to give them the job of giving out the food; that was too easy. I wanted to put them at the entrance to our feeding center and tell them that their job was to count the first five hundred kids who came in and then say to the others, "Sorry. No more food. Go on, leave."

How would you handle that? Could you look a starving Haitian kid in the face and say, "I'm sorry, but you have to starve because we've run out of food"?

I don't want to put a guilt trip on you, but there is something wrong with us when we can spend so much on ourselves, and be so insensitive to the fact that there are five hundred million children in the world today who are suffering from hunger and malnutrition.

When you become possessed by Jesus, when the mind of Christ takes over your mind, when you begin to think His thoughts, when you start to feel what He feels, you will enter into His sufferings. Then the things that break the heart of Jesus will break your heart.

There is an incredible slum I wish you could visit. It is like thousands of such slums throughout the Third World. It is only a hundred acres in size, yet forty thousand people are squeezed into it. They live in squalor that defies imagination. There are suffering and death everywhere. Amid those suffering people is a priest who tries to serve them with a dedication worthy of sainthood. One morning that priest woke me and my students at six in the morning. He said, "I want you to see something." We followed him through the mud paths that separated the lean-to shacks of that hellhole. There was a flu epidemic in progress. When flu hits an American community, children miss school. In an impoverished Third World country, when malnourished children get the flu, they die. As we made our way through the mud paths of that slum, we saw mothers come out of those shacks carrying in their arms the tiny corpses of children who had died during the night. We followed those mothers as they walked with their priests to the edge of the slum where we dug a ditch. And into that ditch we laid the emaciated bodies of those tiny babies, side by side. We heard the mothers scream and cry as only bereaved mothers can scream and cry. The priest said what he had to say and ended with a prayer.

Then we began to shovel the dirt over those tiny dead bodies. As I looked across the ditch, I noticed one of my students, a great big basketball player. I had never seen him cry before, but his lower lip was trembling, his fists were clenched, and tears were running down his cheeks. Something inside of me said, "Blessed are they that mourn, for they shall be comforted." Indeed, there is a comfort that is only for those who enter into the sufferings of Jesus.

There is joy in this walk with Jesus, but there is agony too. To be possessed by Jesus is to begin to care about people as you have never, ever cared for them before. Their hurts will become your hurts, and their agonies will become your agonies, because that's what it means to be in Jesus and to have Jesus in you.

He will not only strengthen you to do His will, He will change your emotional makeup so that you will begin to feel His feelings.

You don't have to go across the sea to find hurting people. You can find them right in your own backyard. One day when I was in my office, my mother called. I'm a good Italian boy and when an Italian mother calls, the Italian boy listens. Mom had some bad news: Mrs. Kilpatrick had died. She was a dear, wonderful woman who had lived on my street in West Philadelphia. She had done so many beautiful things for me when I was growing up, like taking me to art museums and concerts. Actually, she had almost single-handedly helped to broaden my cultural horizons. My mother said, "The least you can do is show some respect and go to the funeral." So I went. Italians are big on respect.

The next day I got into the car, drove to the funeral home, and arrived right at two o'clock. I bounded up the steps, ran inside, took a deep breath, sat down, and bowed my head in prayer. When I lifted my head and looked around, I realized that other than the elderly lady to my immediate left, there wasn't anybody else in the whole room. I peered over the edge of the casket and I knew that the man in that box did not look like Mrs. Kilpatrick. Then I realized that I had gotten into the wrong funeral.

I was just about to make my move and get out when the old woman grabbed my arm. Then she looked at me painfully and said, "You were his friend, weren't you?" What would you do? Come on now, what would you say? "No, I didn't know your husband. I wandered in here by accident. Your husband didn't have any friends!"

No way! You couldn't do that and neither could I. I hate to admit this, but for the record I've got to tell you. I lied. I said, "Yeah, he was a good man. Everybody liked him," or something like that. I went through the entire funeral with that old woman. It was just the two of us. And after the funeral, we went out to the cemetery, which seemed like a hundred miles away. I stood at the edge of the grave and watched as the casket was lowered into it. In the East we always throw a flower on the casket. So she threw her flower, and I threw mine.

We got back in the limousine and headed back for town. As we neared the funeral home, I said, "Mrs. King, there's something I've got to tell you. I want to be your friend and we can't have a friendship unless I tell the truth. I'm afraid I have to tell you that I really didn't know your husband. I came to this funeral by accident." She took hold of my hand and squeezed it so tightly it hurt. Then she said slowly, "You'll never, ever, ever know how much your being with me today meant to me."

And on the way home, I realized I had done something of great significance. At first I couldn't figure out what it was. I hadn't witnessed to her or given her the Four Spiritual Laws. I hadn't given her a tract or a Gospel of John. Then this verse came to me: "Bear ye one another's burdens, and so fulfill the law of Christ" (Gal. 6:2).

When you become a Christian, you will develop a sensitivity to people who are hurting. You will want to share the hurts of those who suffer. You will know not only the joy of Jesus, but you will also know the sorrow that Jesus knows.

There is one last thing that you will come to know in being surrendered to Jesus. You will come to know His anger. That's right—*anger*. Jesus gets angry. There are all kinds of things that make Him angry. Poverty makes Him angry; political oppression makes Him angry; economic injustice makes Him angry; racism and sexism make Him angry. All of these demonic social conditions make Him angry. It is time for you to realize that when you become a Christian, the things that are wrong with this world will make you angry too. They will anger you so much that you will say, "Jesus, I am ready to join with

You in trying to destroy the works of the devil." That's what it says in 1 John 3:8—we are called to destroy the works of Satan.

Racism is one of the ugliest works of Satan. Racism in this country has resulted in hatred between some black and white people. That is the work of Satan. And when racism manifests itself, Jesus calls His disciples to anger.

I have a friend by the name of Clarence Jordan. Actually he's dead now, but I talk about him as still being a friend because I believe that even though he is dead, he is more alive today than he has ever been. Clarence once described going to a church to conduct a revival meeting in the back hills of South Carolina. This was back in the mid-1950s when segregation was practiced and racism was all too common in that region.

When he took his place behind the pulpit to preach his first sermon, Clarence looked over the crowd and, much to his surprise, the congregation was made up of a mixture of black and white folks. He couldn't believe what his eyes saw. He wondered how such a thing could happen.

Following the service, he asked the old hillbilly preacher who was the pastor of the church, "How did you get this way?" The old hillbilly preacher answered, "What way?" Clarence said, "You know, integrated. Blacks and whites together. Has this come about because of the Supreme Court decision on integration?" The old preacher said, "Supreme Court? What's the Supreme Court got to do with Christians?"

Good question. Maybe the people of the world need the Supreme Court to tell them that discrimination is wrong. But the Bible has already spoken to Christians on such matters.

"Come on!" said Clarence. "You know you've got a weird church here. How did you get it to be this way?"

"Well," said the preacher, "they used to have about twenty members in this church when the last preacher died."

"But there are hundreds and hundreds of people out there now," Clarence said. "That's right," agreed the preacher. "When that old preacher died, they couldn't get a new preacher no how. So, after about two months, I told the deacons that I'd be the new preacher. Since they didn't have anybody else, they let me preach.

"I got up the next Sunday, opened the Bible, put my finger down, and landed on that verse that says, 'In Christ there is neither Jew nor Greek, bond nor free, male nor female . . . all are one in Christ Jesus.' So I preached on that," the old preacher said. "I told them people how Jesus makes all kinds of people one. When I finished, the deacons told me they wanted to talk to me in the back room. And when the deacons got there, they told me they didn't want to hear that kind of preaching no more."

Clarence asked, "What did you do then?"

The old hillbilly said, "I *fired* them deacons. I mean if a deacon's not going to 'deke,' he ought to be fired."

Clarence was amazed. "How come the deacons didn't fire you?"

"They never hired me," replied the preacher. "You know, once I found out what bothered them people, I gave it to them every week; I put the knife in the same place, Sunday after Sunday."

Clarence said, "Did they put up with it?"

"Not really," the preacher answered. "I preached that church down to four people. Sometimes revival begins not when we get a lot of new people into the church, but when we get some of the old people out of the church. If people are going to stand in the way of the moving of God, it's better they be gone. After that we only let Christians in this church."

"How can you tell who the Christians are?" Clarence wanted to know.

"Well," answered that old preacher, "down here we're taught since we're knee-high to a grasshopper that there's a difference between black folk and white folk and they shouldn't mix. But we know that when people get saved then all of that garbage is gone. We know that we got Christians on our hands when all that stuff about race is taken out of folks' hearts. Well, when we got some Christians in this church, it started to grow and grow. And that's how we got to the way we are now."

That evening, Clarence Jordan went to spend the night at

the home of a member of the church. That member was a graduate of Yale with a Ph.D. in English literature who was on the faculty at the University of South Carolina. The man drove seventy miles to go to that church. That night Clarence asked that young, sophisticated member of the intelligentsia, "Why do you go to that church? Why do you go to hear that old hillbilly preach? You're used to good English and that preacher can't utter a sentence without making a grammatical error."

The man answered sternly, "Sir, I go to that church because that man preaches the gospel."

The gospel is not simply that you go to heaven when you die; the gospel is much more than that. The gospel is that Jesus is here and now, and He will enter into your life, and He will remove a lot of things from your consciousness that this culture has bred into you. The gospel will make you love people you've never loved before. This is what that hillbilly preacher knew, which a lot of people who think they are Christians have never learned.

When you become a Christian, Jesus will invade your life and make you into somebody He can use to change the world. Through you, He will challenge racism. Through you, Jesus will attack sexism, poverty, and militarism. That was never taught to me when I was growing up. I never heard that I would be an instrument that God could use to change the world. All I was told was that being a Christian meant I would go to heaven when I died. I was never told that the primary reason Jesus saved me was to make me into somebody whom He could use to change the world into the kind of world He willed for it to be when He created it. I was never told that Christians are called to be angry with the injustices that anger God.

I must admit that Christianity may make you into an angry young woman or an angry young man. That's because you will find intolerable many of the things that people around you all too readily accept. Little by little, God will change you into an agent of His revolution in history. I know what you are think-ing: "Hey, Tony! That's a *big* world out there. Little folks like me can't change it." If you think that, you're wrong. We *can* change it. God wants to equip us to do it.

I want you to dream dreams. I want you to have visions. I want you to believe that this same Jesus who died on the cross for your sins two thousand years ago is with you right now. I want you to know that He wants to invade your life; that He wants to take possession of you; that He wants to use you to do His will. He truly wants to do this. He wants to use you to touch the lives of people who are hurt, to bring joy to people who are sad. He wants to make you into an agent fighting for His great revolution. He wants to begin to change the world through you.

And when you accept Jesus into your life, things will begin to happen on a scale that will surprise you. You, like the "man from la Mancha," will "dream the impossible dream." You will "fight the unbeatable foe." You will fight with your "last ounce of courage." You will go "where the brave dare not go."

God wants to do great things through you. I don't want you just to believe in Him; I want you to be committed to Him. I want you to be ready to say, "Jesus, I'm ready to do what You would do if You were in my shoes. Come into my life and empower me to do it. I want to know Your joy. I want to be a person through whom You can express Your love to a world that needs You."

Young person, the world needs you. And Jesus needs you. Jesus calls you to do His work in His world. Now. Today. Forever!

SETTING A COURSE AND TRAVELING LIGHT

DURING the 1960s, one of the most popular singing groups was the Kingston Trio. They had a hit song that went like this:

> They're rioting in Africa.
> They're starving in Spain.
> There's hurricanes in Florida,
> And Texas needs rain.
> The whole world is festering,
> With unhappy souls.
> The French hate the Germans,

And the Germans hate the Poles.

The Italians hate the Yugoslavs.

The South Africans hate the Dutch.

And I don't like anybody very much.

But we can be grateful,

And thankful and proud,

For man is endowed with a mushroom-shaped cloud.

And we can be certain,

That some happy day.

Someone will set the spark off,

And we will all be blown away.

They're rioting in Africa,

There's strife in Iran,

What nature doesn't do to us,

Will be done by our fellow man.

That song communicated an important fact, something with which we all must deal sometime. *The world is a mess*. We must not only face that fact but we must realize that God has called us to join with Him to try to set the world right. That's why Jesus came into the world. He came because He loves our world and He wants to call together an army of people through whom He can change it back into the wonderful world He willed for it to be when He created it.

When we pray the Lord's Prayer, we are praying for a

personal and social revolution through which the transformation of our world will become a reality. There is a plea for a revolution when we pray, "Thy kingdom come. Thy will be done in earth, as it is in heaven" (Matt. 6:10). Jesus has plans for creating His kingdom right here on earth just as it is in heaven. He wants this world to be the same kind of wonderful place that heaven is. He wants His will to be done, His kingdom to come, right here on this planet, and He calls us to join Him in the task of making His will a historical reality. We are the people who have been called by God to join with Him to change the world.

I want to make this as clear as I know how: I want to emphatically assert that Jesus desperately wants you to allow Him to work through you to begin to change His world into the world He wills for it to be.

I know what some of you are thinking: "Change the world? Me? How could someone like me possibly be used by God to change the world? The world is enormous. Its population is in the billions. Its problems seem unsolvable. Its institutions seem unchangeable. I wouldn't even know how a world revolution could begin."

Well, first of all, the changing of the world begins with people like you and me speaking out and witnessing to what Jesus has done in our personal lives and inviting other people to allow Jesus to change them too. A lot of people probably don't realize that God's revolution begins with personal evangelism. To change the world, we have to start by changing people. This world is not going to be changed unless the people's hearts and minds and souls are changed. Jesus' plan is to change people and through them to change the world. That's where you come in. You are called to win people to Jesus and to recruit volunteers for His movement. Through the witness of Christians like you and me, He will raise up an army of agents through which He can infiltrate and change every sector and institution of our world.

For ten years I taught at the University of Pennsylvania, a large Ivy League university. While I was there I taught an advanced seminar class. We met weekly for several hours and we talked about all kinds of really heavy stuff. We covered everything from Einstein's theory of relativity to the meaning of life. And one night our discussion got pretty religious. We got to talking about God.

When the lecture was over, some of the guys in the seminar said, "Hey! Come back to our apartment. We want to talk to you some more." So I went back to their apartment and we talked and talked until about two in the morning.

Now, you can't get me talking to people that long without talking about Jesus. Little by little the discussion focused on the Lord. What was neat was that these guys really hadn't heard much about Jesus before. I know some of you are going to have trouble accepting the fact that there really are highly educated people out there who haven't heard much about Jesus. But it's true. There are. As it turned out, a couple of the guys came from Jewish backgrounds. So when I talked to them about Jesus, it was all new stuff to them. They were fascinated. Most of them had never had an in-depth discussion with any-one who had any acquaintance with the New Testament.

We talked and talked and talked. The following week they invited me back to their apartment for another discussion. They invited me again the week after that and the week after that. In the course of the semester, one by one, each of the original four guys and the friends they had begun bringing to our Thursday night gatherings became Christians. More than that—they became radically committed Christians. Their zeal for Christ was so intense that they began to have an impact on that campus like you wouldn't believe.

One day I was in the bookstore at the university, and one of the leaders of the Hebrew Association came in and looked at me and said, "Campolo, I don't know whether to bless you or to curse you." I said, "Look, if I've got a choice, I'll take the bless-ing! What's bothering you?"

He said, "You know that group of students that gets together on Thursday nights? They never used to come to our meetings before. Now they come every week." I said, "That's terrific." He said, "That is terrific. Not only do they come, but they're running around the university rounding up all of the other Jewish kids and bringing them along with them. The place is packed on Friday nights!"

I said, "You ought to be happy with that." He said, "I am. But this is what I don't like. At our meetings we always divide into small groups for discussion and your boys spread themselves out into all of those different discussion groups. And do you know what they're doing in my synagogue?"

Actually, by this point, I didn't have to be told, but I asked anyway. He told me that they were telling the other people in the group about Jesus. "Campolo, you want to do your evangelizing? Do your evangelizing, I got nothing against it. Just stay out of my synagogue, understand?"

When I got to the meeting the next Thursday, I said, "Hey, guys, that was really terrific! I mean, that was pretty amazing! Right up there in the synagogue, you were telling people about Jesus! Man! What a neat way to do it! Where did you come up with that idea?" One of the guys looked up at me and said, "From the Book of Acts, baby!"

These new Christians witnessed wherever and whenever they could. They knew that part of their mission was to win people to Jesus. They understood better than most church people that Jesus "saves" us in order that He might use us to reach others with His message and gradually build up a movement through which He can change the world.

When it comes to talking to people about Jesus, nobody can do it better than you. I was the pastor of a church for a while but it wasn't the lifestyle for me. I wish it had been. I would love being the pastor of a church. But being a pastor requires a patience and quality of character that I lack. One of my basic problems was that I never could resist a good one-liner. For instance, one Sunday a lady walking out of the church said to me, "Reverend, do you know how many grammatical errors you made in the prayer this morning?" Before I could catch myself, I said, "Lady, I wasn't talking to you anyway." It wiped her out—but it didn't help my pastoral image.

During the time I was a pastor, I tried to witness for Jesus to people in the community, but it never worked out too well. They always viewed me as "the clergyman." Everywhere I went, people's defenses went up.

I can remember going up to the barbershop each week. (This may seem funny to those of you who know how baldheaded I am.) And every time I walked in, I seemed to interrupt the joking and laughing going on among the other men who were waiting their turns for haircuts. As soon as I'd walk in, the barber would say, "Good morning, *Reverend*!" and everybody would freeze. They would quickly slip those semipornographic magazines under their seats and fold their hands. Then the conversation would always get going slowly. "Nice weather we're having." "Yes, I'm glad it didn't snow. It's too hot to shovel snow," or something stupid like that. The only good thing was that they would let me go next in line for my haircut just to get me out of there.

You see, people tend to get all phony when the clergyman is around. That's why those of you who aren't ministers have an opportunity to witness for Jesus in a way that clergy-types cannot.

Have you heard the story about the little kid who unknowingly comes home during a pastoral call? He doesn't realize that the pastor is there. He just sees his mom and he comes running into his house holding a dead rat by the tail. He says, "Look, Mom! Look at this rat I caught out behind the barn! I smashed its head in with a baseball bat! I threw rocks at it! I stomped on it! I spit on it and I, I, I . . ." and he looks up and sees the minister, clears his throat and says, "And, and, and then the dear Lord called it home!"

This ability to change whenever "the Reverend" shows up is one of the reasons why when it comes to witnessing for Jesus, nobody can do it better than you can. People do not set up the same defenses against you as they do against clergy-types. They don't act phony around you as they do around professional religious people. You may be thinking right about now, "I don't know whether I can. I don't know whether I have what it takes to really share Jesus with others." Of course you do. If Jesus has done something in your life, all you have to do is share that with other people. If you love Jesus enough, you'll always find a way to get the story told.

Some time ago, I was invited to be a counselor at a junior high camp. I don't know how many of you people out there reading this book are Roman Catholics, but that old Roman Catholic theology is right: there is a purgatory. It is junior high camp—a place between heaven and hell where people go to suffer for their sins.

I have never met meaner kids in my life than at this junior high camp. Don't get me wrong. I love junior high kids individually, but the gang at this junior high camp was really bad. Something must happen to kids in a group at camp. They get mean. Let me tell you, *these* kids at *this* junior high camp turned *really* mean. Their meanness was focused on an unfortunate kid named Billy. Billy really broke my heart because he had been born with a whole host of birth defects. He had cerebral palsy and his brain was unable to exercise proper control over the movements of his body or his speech. The other kids mocked him. They called him "spastic." Billy would walk across the grounds of the camp in his disjointed manner, and the others would line up behind him, imitating him and mimicking his every movement. They thought this was funny. It was the worst kind of junior high cruelty I had ever seen.

One day I watched as Billy asked one of the boys a question: "Which way is the craft shop?" The other boy twisted up grotesquely, pointed a dozen different ways and said, "That way!" I felt like punching out that mean kid. How could he be so cruel to a handicapped boy?

The level of meanness reached its lowest point on a Wednesday morning. Billy's cabin had been assigned the morning devotions for that camp of 150 kids. All of the boys in his cabin had voted for Billy to be the speaker. I knew, and they knew, that he couldn't do it; they just wanted to get him up there so that they could mock him and laugh. They thought it would be fun to watch "spastic Billy" try to deliver a devotional talk. I was irate. And I was livid. I was seething with anger as little Billy got up out of his seat and limped his way to the platform. You could hear the titters of mocking laughter and sneering going through the group. I could not remember ever being so angry. What was amazing was that the ridicule of the boys didn't stop that little guy. He took his place behind the rostrum and started to speak. It took Billy almost ten tortured minutes to say, "Je-sus loves meee! Je-Je-Je-sus loves meee! And I love Je-Je-Jesus." And when he finished there was dead silence. I looked over my shoulder, and there were junior high school boys shaking and trembling and crying all over the place.

A revival broke out in that camp and kids turned their lives over to Jesus. A host of junior high boys committed their lives to Christian service. I wish I had kept count of how many ministers I have met as I travel across this country who have told me that they gave their lives to Jesus because of the witness of a "spastic" kid named Billy.

If God could use him with all of his limitations, what makes you think that God can't use you to touch the lives of other people? If God can transform the lives of people through the likes of little Billy, don't you dare tell me He can't do great things through you.

I hope I have made it clear that when we talk about God's revolution, our first responsibility is to witness for Christ. God's revolution begins with people like you and me winning others to this movement called Christianity. God's revolution is dependent upon having a host of agents who can be deployed in every sector of society. Then these revolutionaries not only can share the message of Jesus but can begin to bring about the kinds of changes that God wills for society. Change agents for God's revolution are needed in every social institution and business. They are needed in every school, every university, every corporate office, every labor union, every television studio, every farm, every state legislature, and most important—in every family. Many people underrate the importance of what goes on in the home, but I am convinced that of all the social institutions that must be brought under the lordship of Christ, none take precedence over the family.

A case in point: my wife is a really neat person, the most articulate person I know. She can really talk; she has a way with words that staggers my imagination. And I love it whenever we're at some social gathering and somebody, like some woman lawyer, comes and says, in the most condescending voice, "And what is it that you do, my dear?" Most of you reading this book probably aren't married, so you might not realize that such a question is often a disguised put-down of homemakers by those who think that the only significant work in society is in some professional vocation.

My wife has the greatest comeback in the world, something you can use when you get married. When somebody asks, "And what is it that you do, my dear?" she answers, "I am socializing two *Homo sapiens* into the dominant values of the Judeo-Christian tradition in order that they might be instruments for the transformation of the social order into the kind of eschatological utopia that God willed from the beginning of creation." Then she usually looks back at the other person and asks, "And what is it that *you* do?" Often the reply, "I'm a lawyer," is made in a very subdued voice.

I don't know what your job will be, whether you will be a lawyer, a musician, a laborer, an artist, a businessperson, or a government worker. But if you are a committed Christian, that is, if you are committed to the revolution God is carrying out in our world, you should be asking, "How can I change things where I work so that things will be set up more in accord with the will of God? How can I restructure the organization of my workplace so that the principles of God's justice are put into action?" Those of you who will be housewives or househusbands ought to be asking the same kinds of questions. You should be asking, "How can I change things in the house so that my family functions more in accord with the will of God? How can I promote the kind of family life that will express the revolutionary principles that Jesus outlined for us in the Scriptures?"

When I used the word "househusband," I did so for a reason. Being a *househusband* is becoming a real possibility these days. It's happening everywhere. In many families wives are securing jobs outside the house and husbands are opting to become homemakers. I can just read the thoughts of some of the guys who are reading this book. *Househusband?* Wouldn't that be terrific? Play tennis all morning, watch soap operas all afternoon.

If that's what you think, you don't know what keeping house is really like, guys. It's a jungle in there. You'll work harder keeping house with a couple of kids under your feet than you would ever have to work in any factory or office. You should try doing housework sometime. What's worse is that there are a thousand and one put-downs to be endured in that job. For instance, it's hard enough to keep house without having television ads constantly reminding you of ways in which you might be failing. Try the ad in which a housewife is reduced to tears by a whining voice chanting, "Ring around the collar, ring around the collar!"

She's being condemned because her detergent didn't get rid of the dirt inside the collar of her husband's shirt. The ad never asks the right question, *"Why doesn't he wash his neck?"*

In the home, in the marketplace, in the schools, in government everywhere—God needs people who will implement the principles of His revolution and work to change the world. Ask yourself, "What needs to change at the place where I live and work if God is to be pleased?" Then commit yourself to effect that change.

I had a friend who understood that being a Christian was not only telling others about Jesus, but changing the way things happened at the job. He understood that his work style was to express his commitment to God's revolution. He realized that he was supposed to implement in his vocational activities the principles of the kingdom of God and thus undermine the present social order with the new order that is in accord with God's Word.

This friend and I were in graduate school together. He went on to teach at Trenton State University and I went to teach at Eastern College. After teaching at Trenton State for about three weeks, he walked into the dean's office and said, "I'm not coming back tomorrow. I'm quitting this job. I thought you should know."

The dean said, "You can't walk out on a teaching position in the middle of a semester."

My friend responded, "Watch me!"

Later his mother telephoned me and said, "Tony, you have to go and talk to Charlie. He quit his job. He's a Ph.D. in English literature and if he doesn't teach, what can he possibly do?" Now, I have to admit, that *is* a good question. What do you do with a Ph.D. in English if you don't teach?

So I hunted him up. I found him living in an attic apartment in Hamilton Square, New Jersey. I've got to admit, I liked the apartment. He had travel posters on his walls, shelves and shelves of books, a stereo; he had the whole "with it" scene. As I walked into the apartment he said, "Sit down, man. Sit down." So I sat down—in one of those beanbag chairs. Did you ever sit in one of those things? It was like a giant ameba. That chair threatened to devour me right on the spot. As I sat down there in that chair, half-consumed and half-digested, he looked at me with a Buddha-like smile and said, "I quit, Tony. I quit."

I said, "I know you quit, Charlie. Why did you quit?"

He said, "I can't teach, man. I can't teach those people. Every time I walked into that class and gave a lecture, I died a little."

Now I can understand that. I'm a teacher. I know what it is like to go into a class and share truth. Truth! Real truth! Truth wrenched from existential suffering! Truth gleaned from the pains of human existence! And after I have shared truth with my students, after I've let every nerve and sinew tingle with the excitement of grappling with ultimate truth, some kid on the last row raises his hand and asks, "Do we have to know this for the final?" And I die a little bit.

So I empathized with Charlie. I understood him. And it wasn't long before I realized that I couldn't dissuade him from his decision to give up teaching. Finally, I said, "What are you doing now? How are you feeding yourself?"

He said, "I'm a mailman."

I said, "That's terrific. A Ph.D. mailman."

He shot back, "There aren't too many of us!"

I couldn't change his mind, so I came back with the old Protestant work ethic thing. I said, "Charlie, if you're gonna be a mailman, be the *best* mailman you can be."

He looked at me with a silly grin and said, "I'm a lousy mailman."

I asked, "What do you mean, you're a lousy mailman?"

He answered, "Everybody else gets the mail delivered by one o'clock; I never get back until about five-thirty or six."

"What takes you so long?" I wanted to know.

He said, "I visit! That's why it takes so long. You wouldn't believe how many people on my route never got visited until I became the mailman. But I've got this problem, I can't sleep at nights."

I asked, "Why can't you sleep?"

He said, "Who can sleep after drinking twenty cups of coffee?"

I began to get the image of this mailman on the job. He was no ordinary mailman. I could picture him going from door to door and at each home giving more than the mail. I could see him visiting solitary widows, counseling troubled teenagers, joking with lonely old men. I could see him delivering the mail in a way that was revolutionary for the people on his route.

He's the only mailman I know that on his birthday, the people on his route get together, hire out a gym, and throw a party for him. They love him because he's a mailman who expresses the love of Jesus everywhere he goes. In his own subtle way, my friend Charlie is changing his world, changing the lives of people, touching them where they are, making a difference in their lives. It may not sound like much, but that man who is delivering mail as Jesus would deliver mail is an agent of God who is changing the world.

Just as a homemaker doing the job as Jesus would want it done becomes a person through whom God can change things in this world; just as a mailman delivering mail like Jesus would deliver it is a revolutionary, so can you as students begin to bring about the new world which God wills by the ways in which you function at school. Young people, do you realize what your opportunity is? You have a chance to go to your school and share Jesus Christ, not just in words, but in the way you treat people at that school. You can be an agent through which God can begin to change your school into His kind of school.

A lot of people are upset these days because the Supreme Court has ruled against having Bible readings or prayer in public schools. They won't let preachers talk about Jesus in school assemblies anymore either. Now maybe the Supreme Court's keeping religion out of the school curriculum is a good thing. You see, it puts the responsibility right where it ought to be— on you guys and girls who go to those schools. You are the ones who must carry Jesus into your classrooms. You must be God's agents. You must reveal Christ to the people at your school. You can do it by the way you conduct yourselves, by the way in which you treat other people, and in how you talk to your teachers/professors. You help to further God's revolution by the ways in which you change things at your school. Since the Supreme Court's ruling, there is no question but that you are the agents of God's revolution at whatever school you attend.

We witness by what we *say*, but we also witness and exercise an influence for change by what we *do*. It's part of the whole theme of being an instrument of God in the world.

As a sociologist I will never underestimate the importance of the "foolishness of preaching," as the Scripture says—converting people to Jesus. I know how working for change in the places where you are employed, going to school, and living can influence society. However, I also know that we must do more than these things if we are to change the world. Furthermore, the Bible declares that we are called to do more than tell people about Jesus and exercise an influence for the kingdom of God.

For those of you who are willing to get a little intellectual, let me tell you what a Dutch theologian named Hendrick Berkhof has to teach us from the Scriptures. Berkhof wrote a whole book explaining a phrase that is used over and over by the apostle Paul: principalities and powers. If you know the New Testament, you know that phrase. We read in Ephesians 6:12, "For we wrestle not against flesh and blood, but against principalities, against powers, against the rulers of the darkness of this world."

That verse tells us that in the process of living the Christian life we must struggle against Satan on two levels. First of all, we must fight against what Satan is trying to do to us through "the flesh." You guys reading this know what that is all about, right? I don't know about girls; I can only write from a male perspective and speak from experience. But I do know about the guys. I do know that guys have great problems overcoming what Satan is trying to do to them through the flesh.

The truth of the matter is that we all have flesh problems. Sigmund Freud understood this when he said that there are sexual urges that overpower our psyches. Freud discovered that the sexual powers in the normal person are so awesome that nothing—not even cultural restraints—can defuse or negate them.

Of course, Sigmund Freud didn't know what Jesus could do.

He did not know that Christ can enable an individual to control his or her sexual drives and direct them into constructive and humanizing love relationships. Freud did not know that with Jesus an individual is able to overcome the destructive tendencies of sexuality. If I know anything about the teenage years, it is this: without the help of Jesus, sex can destroy you.

You all saw kids in your high school who messed up their lives because of sex. It really can ruin your life, your dreams, and your future. I don't have to paint you pictures to let you know what can happen when sexual drives get out of control.

We all must struggle against the sexual tendencies inherent in the flesh, but the good news is that Jesus joins us in this struggle and helps us to overcome the demonic designs for our sex lives. When our flesh is weak, when we find that we cannot overcome sexual temptation, then we know that we can invite Him to work through us and strengthen us. We can ask Him to make us conquerors over the flesh.

I don't know about the rest of you guys, but I know in my own life that I get turned on easily. Some of you are thinking, "Doc, you're supposed to be a spiritual guy. You're not supposed to get turned on." Well, I do. I get turned on for a very simple reason. I'm human. So was Jesus. And what's more, Jesus got turned on. You say, "Not Jesus! That's sacrilegious!"

But remember, the Bible says that He was tempted in all ways as we are tempted, but He had within Himself the power of the Father. Because He depended on the strength of His father, He was able to overcome all and any temptations and remain "without sin." That same power is available to us, so when in fact you and I do succumb to the lust of the flesh, we can never say, "Oh well, I'm only human." God meant for you to be more than human; in your humanness He meant for you to depend upon His power to overcome the lusts of the flesh.

Not only does He want us to overcome the flesh, but Ephesians 6:12 tells us that He also wants us to overcome the *principalities and powers*. Hendrick Berkhof tries to explain to us what the apostle Paul means when he uses that phrase: Principalities and power are the societal forces and institutional structures that influence us and constrain our behavior. They include the social institutions to which we belong and which have so much to do with what we are and how we act. Principalities and powers are all of those elements of the culture in which we live that condition what we do. Are we *really* influenced by the principalities and powers, you ask?

You bet we are. For instance, television is one of the principalities and powers, and no one would question the fact that television molds us. Motion pictures are principalities and powers, and they mold us too. As a matter of fact, I would say that most of you reading this book are molded by the media far more than you are molded by the Holy Spirit. That's something we have to change. We must stop being controlled by the media. We must struggle to allow ourselves more and more to come under the control of the Holy Spirit. It's easy to see that we are media creations by the way we dress, the way we talk, the way we act—almost everything we do is influenced by the media. The apostle Paul tells us that we must struggle against the influence of this principality and power.

Does the school system mold us? Of course it does. Does the political system mold us? Of course it does. Do large industries mold our behavior? Of course they do. The Bible teaches us, particularly in Paul's Epistle to the Colossians, that Satan is able to use the principalities and powers to influence us to do things that are contrary to the will of God. As Christians we are called upon not to conform to what the demonically controlled principalities and powers condition us to do. The Bible says in Romans 12:2, "Be not conformed to this world: but be ye transformed by the renewing of your mind, that ye may prove what is that good, and acceptable, and perfect, will of God."

However, as Christian revolutionaries, we are called not only to resist the influences of the principalities and powers but to take them over and bring them under the lordship of Christ. Or, to put it more simply, we are commissioned by God to change each and every social institution of our society so that they all function as God wants them to function and influence people in the way God wants them influenced. Let me tell you about one attempt by some Christians to do just that.

A group of my students became very, very upset with one large corporation, Gulf and Western Industries. While we were doing some missionary work in the Dominican Republic, we became aware of the fact that this huge, multinational corporation was taking land that should have been used to grow food for needy people in that poor country—and using that land to grow sugar.

As you probably know, sugar is bad for you to begin with. So is coffee. So is tobacco. You should know that if all of the land in the world that is presently being used to grow sugar, coffee, and tobacco—all of which poison our systems—were used to grow food, we could cut malnutrition in the Third World by almost 50 percent.

Anyway, we were upset with Gulf and Western because we saw that they were growing sugar for people in the United States on land that we felt should have been used to grow food for needy Dominican peasants.

I think you'll find our method of protest interesting. There were eleven of us, and each of us bought one share of stock in the company. I don't know how many millions of shares of stock there are in Gulf and Western, but we owned eleven of them. It is important for you to realize that you only need one share to go to the annual stockholders meeting. So each of us "stockholders" went to the meeting and we said our piece.

We were probably somewhat arrogant about it, but we

really laid into them! "Hey! We don't like the way you are running this company! This company belongs to God." In private confrontations following that meeting, we met with some of the company's top executives, and we told from the Bible the story of a certain man who had a vineyard. The man went away on a long trip, but the people he left in charge of the vineyard didn't run it right. He sent messengers, but they wouldn't listen to the messengers. Then he sent his son, but the people put him to death. Jesus ends that parable with the question, "What then should the owner of the vineyard do to the unfaithful stewards when he returns?"

We told all of that and more. "This company belongs, in the end, to God. You are His stewards. He doesn't like the way you are running the company, so we have come as messengers. You had better listen to us, or God is going to come and get you."

Now that was sheer arrogance. Looking back on our behavior, I have to admit we weren't at all Christlike or *even fair*. But what followed those encounters was incredible. We found out that the leaders of that company weren't bad men. It took us a while to come to grips with that. But little by little we became convinced that they were good and decent men. The more we talked, the more we interacted and the more we became aware that they wanted to do what was right. In our talks with them they convinced us that they wanted Gulf and Western to be an instrument for good in the Dominican Republic.

About a year and a half after our discussions with Gulf and Western began, I got a call from one of the executives of that corporation. He said, "Tomorrow we're going to have a press conference and part of the reason we're holding the press conference is to make an announcement about some of the issues we discussed with you. We want you to be among the first to know what's going to happen."

And as I sat there dumbfounded, that executive told me they were going to announce that Gulf and Western was going to do the following: They would test the soil that made up their landholdings in the Dominican Republic and determine what land could be used to grow food. That land would then be shifted from the production of sugar to the production of food. Second, the company would make a commitment to build forty thousand new housing units for the sugar workers so that they would no longer have to live in the slums. Third, Gulf and Western would provide educational programs and health programs, particularly in the eastern half of the country where their operations were located. The spokesman went on to say that his corporation had made a commitment of $100 million to be spent over the next five years in order to make all the promises a reality. Now *that's* incredible.

Don't tell me corporations can't change. Don't tell me the system is evil and beyond redemption. I think that if we go to corporate executives, hopefully without arrogance, and with reasonable expectations of what needs to be changed and why, calling upon them to respond to the things that the Bible teaches, their responses might exceed our expectations.

The problem with us is that we all know what to say to drunks, alcoholics, drug addicts, and criminals. They are beneath us. But we don't know how to talk to the leaders of the "principalities and powers." We don't have the guts to challenge those who hold positions of power to try to change the political and economic structures of our society in order that they might function more in accord with the will of God. Jesus calls us to be agents of change, to participate with Him in changing the world into the kind of world He wants it to be.

I want you to become a revolutionary for Jesus. When I ask you to be a revolutionary, I don't mean that I want you to get a gun and do something violent. I'm asking you to do something else. I'm asking you to seriously consider—right this very minute—going to some Third World country to do something for Jesus among people who have real needs. Some of you should consider being servants of God to the poor. All of you should give serious consideration to the possibility of becoming missionaries. I don't know if you realize that God not only wants to make America better; He wants to transform people and "principalities and powers" in every nation of the world. He wants His revolutionaries at work everywhere.

You are growing up in the United States of America and

that's good news. This is a fantastic country. The bad news is—are you ready for this?—suburban America does not need you. When you graduate, what are you going to do? Are you thinking of becoming a schoolteacher? Why not go to one of our country's many inner city schools, rather than a private school where the teachers are plenty? The inner city school system is desperately in need of good teachers. Or how about going to teach in an entirely different country, such as a place where the teachers are scarce? So many places are in need of good teachers—find out where those places are and go.

Are you thinking of becoming a lawyer? We've got too many lawyers now. We have one lawyer for every four hundred people in the United States. Graduates from law schools are hard-pressed in their attempts to find law firms to employ them. Have you considered being a doctor among the poor in Third World countries or in urban America?

I could go on and on. It is the same in many other fields. America is becoming overcrowded with competent people it can't use. This raises a new question for today's young person. Today's young person must ask not only, "What can I do to best serve Jesus?" He or she must also ask, "Where can I go?" This is something you kids should be thinking about now.

When I was growing up, a missionary speaker would sometimes say to our youth group, "Some of you ought to consider going to the mission field and the rest will stay at home and support you." In this day and age, I think the reverse should be said. We should tell a typical youth group, "Most of you ought to consider going, and the only people who ought to stay here at home are the people who are really called to do so." I mean, if God is calling you to be a schoolteacher in some cozy suburb of Dallas or New Orleans or Phoenix, you ought to be one. As I said earlier, every school in America is in need of the transforming presence of Christian revolutionaries. If He is calling you to be a lawyer for the poor in New York or Chicago, do it. God needs revolutionaries in the legal profession.

But it seems to me that unless you have a specific call to serve God here in the United States, you have a responsibility to consider going to that place in the world where you are most needed. And where are you most needed today? There's a likelihood that it won't be in the good old, safe United States of America. Why should anybody want to be a schoolteacher some place like suburban Houston or suburban Omaha when he or she could be a schoolteacher in Haiti?

You could be a teacher in a Third World school where children would run and jump all over you, hug you, and kiss you because you were there. You don't see many teachers around here getting hugged and kissed, do you? Why would you want to be a doctor in the United States when you could be in some village in Africa where you would be urgently needed, where you could be an answer to a desperate need?

Each of us has a responsibility to be in the place where we are most needed. Each of us is called to do something heroic for Jesus. You could be a translator of the Scriptures. Imagine going into a tribe that has never had the Bible, learning the language, translating the Bible into that language, teaching the people to read that language, and sharing Jesus with them. From that day on for the rest of their lives, for the rest of their history, whenever members of that tribe quoted John 3:16, it would be because you went there and made it possible.

Wouldn't you like to do something fantastic like that with your life? God needs not one, not ten, not a thousand, but He needs a hundred thousand young people in the United States of America to rise up and go to places where they are desperately needed in the next five years.

After most people graduate from college, they say to themselves, "What am I going to do with myself?" I wish I could tell each of them, *"Do something great for Jesus."*

One last but very important thing: if you are going to be a revolutionary for Jesus, *you've got to change your personal lifestyle.*

One day back in the counterculture years of the 1960s, I was lecturing to my "Introduction to Sociology" class (which numbered several hundred students) when, in the middle of the lecture, a "way out" looking student stood up and shouted, "Bull! Bull! Bull! Bull!"

I yelled, "Sit down, fella! Sit down or you're in serious trouble!"

He shouted back, *"Who cares?"*

I said, "Fella, if you don't sit down I'm going to throw you out of this class."

He yelled back, *"Who cares?"*

I didn't push it. I'm sure that if I had said, "You get thrown out of this class, you're going to be tossed out of this university," he would have yelled, *"Who cares?"* And if I had told him that if he got thrown out of the university, he wouldn't be able to get a job, he would have yelled, *"Who cares?"* And if I had said that without a job he wouldn't have any money to buy all the stuff that America says he ought to have, he would have yelled back at me, *"Who cares?"*

You can't really be a revolutionary agent for Jesus, unless you can look at this world and what it's trying to sell you and yell at the top of your lungs, *"Who cares?"*

Do you really care about the things of this world more than you care about serving Jesus? Let me tell you that as long as you must have what this society has to offer, this society will control you.

I control my students because they want good grades. I can give them good grades; therefore, I have control over them. I can make them read books they don't want to read, and write papers they don't want to write. I can even make them stay up all night studying for tests they don't want to take. That's my power. And do you know why I have that power? Because they want what I can give them.

The American society will control you and you will be its slave until you can say to this society and everything that it has to offer, *"Who cares?"* The cars, the houses, the whole shooting match. If you have them, enjoy them—but if you're going to be a revolutionary for Jesus, you must be the kind of person who can do without any of these things.

I was at a convention of some Mennonite people a while ago. Mennonites, as you may know, are supposed to be pacifists. However, at this convention, an older man made a statement suggesting that perhaps the Mennonites ought to become more like the rest of the people in the world and give up their historical pacifist stance. A young man stood to challenge him.

I can still remember the older man looking back at him sternly and saying, "It's all right for you to talk that way, but one of these days, the Russians will come and take everything you've got."

The young man smiled and said, "If they come, they really can't take everything I've got. You see, when I became a Christian I gave everything I had to Jesus. So if the Russians come and take that stuff, they'll be taking what belongs to Him and that's His problem."

The older man responded, "All right, but don't forget that they can kill you." The young man came back, sharp as a tack, and said, "They can't kill me. You see, mister, I'm already dead."

(The guy was right; that's what the Bible means when it tells us that Christians are "people who have died." When you become a Christian, who you were dies and a new self is born. And the new self that is born can never die.)

The older man looked back at that young man and said, "All right, maybe they can't kill you and maybe they can't take what you have, but they can make you suffer."

Then the young man smiled and said, "When that day comes, I hope I have the grace to repeat the Bible verse, 'Blessed are ye, when men shall revile you, and persecute you, and shall say all manner of evil against you falsely, for my sake. Rejoice, and be exceeding glad: . . . for so persecuted they the prophets which were before you' (Matt. 5:11–12)."

The young man turned to the rest of us and said, "That's the secret of freedom. If you don't have anything, if you're already dead, and if you rejoice when people torture you, then there isn't much they can do to you. There just isn't any way they can threaten you, is there?"

The time may come when we will have to stand up and be counted for Jesus. The question I have to ask you is this: Do you love Jesus enough to be able to say to this world, and all it has to offer, "Who cares?" Will you be as free to follow Jesus as the young man I've just described? Will you be the kind of revolutionary who has committed everything he/she is and has to the cause? If your answer to these questions is "yes," your lifestyle will radically change. You will have a different value system governing your thinking, a different criteria affecting your decisions, and a different set of concerns controlling your spending habits.

Take Christmas, for instance. At Christmas your biggest problem is what to buy for somebody who already has everything. From a radically Christian perspective, you know what to buy for somebody who has everything? Nothing! It would be wild if your parents came down the stairs, looked at all of the kids sitting next to the Christmas tree, and said, "Nobody's getting anything for Christmas this year because everybody's already got everything."

Now that would be the right thing to do, wouldn't it? What right do we have to buy surplus junk at Christmastime, when there are kids who are starving and suffering from malnutrition all over the world? What do you think?

I'm going to lay it on you heavy: say you've got $200 and you want to buy a CD player. On the other hand, you know that the $200 can feed fifty kids in Bangladesh. You can do one of two things. You can buy the CD player, or you can buy food for the hungry kids. Which of the two do you think Jesus would do? Would He buy the CD player, or would He feed the hungry kids? *You know* He'd feed the hungry kids every time. Isn't a Christian someone who tries to do what Jesus would do?

The question each of us must ask is why we continue to spend our money on (as the Scripture says) "things that satisfy you not"?

The time has come for a whole new generation of kids to come along; a generation of kids who do not live for themselves; a generation of kids who want to do something for Jesus; a generation of kids who want to do something for others; a generation of kids who want to do something heroic with their lives.

Years ago I took my son and daughter to Haiti where some of us from Eastern College had helped to develop a school and orphanage. A lot of the money that I could have been spending on my two children had been sent down to Haiti to be spent on the building of this little school, which now had fifty students in it. My kids had never been to the school before. After arriving in Port-au-Prince, we got into the Jeep and drove out to visit the place. After about twenty miles, we ran out of paved road. But we kept traveling. We crossed some fields and eventually came to a clump of trees, on the other side of which was the school. We drove around the trees and there it was. It was December 28 and school was not in session, but I knew what we would find. All fifty kids were there waiting to greet us.

When they saw us, the kids let out a scream! My two children got out of the Jeep and those fifty kids jumped all over them, grabbed them, hugged them, and kissed them. Then they lined up and sang a song that they had learned in English just for us: "Jesus loves the little children, all the children of the world, red and yellow, black and white, they are precious in His sight."

Each of the children took a turn reciting Bible verses for us. Some of them had made us gifts. They were Christmas-tree ornaments made of sticks and string: not much to look at, but somehow very precious.

We gathered up the presents from those grateful children, got into the Jeep and headed back to the capital city. My son and daughter, who were usually very, very talkative, seemed unusually quiet during the return trip. About halfway back to Port-au-Prince, I looked at my son, who seemed rather pensive, and asked him what he was thinking. He said to me, "Dad, there isn't anything you could have done with that money that would have made me happier than I am right now."

Believe me, there is nothing you can do with your life that will make you happier than giving it away to others for Jesus. There is nothing that generates more thrills than using whatever you have in accord with the will of God. When you say, "Jesus, use what I have and am for Your cause and the sake of others," you will discover unparalleled gratification. When you can honestly say, "Lord, begin to change the world through me," you will discover how fulfilling life can be.

I know we're not going to perfect this world; that won't happen until the Second Coming occurs. At the end of history Jesus is coming back to this world and on that day *He* will make the world perfect. However, I believe that God wants to initiate through us a movement that will begin to make the changes which He will complete when He returns. He wants to start His great revolution now—and with you. He wants to know if you will allow Him to use you to begin to change the world. You can go into our government, you can go into our economic structures, you can go into our educational system, or you can go into the emerging Third World countries and become instruments for changing the world. You can use your talents and your financial resources for the cause of Christ. You can know the excitement of participating in God's revolution.

In *The Waste Land*, T. S. Eliot writes: "This is the way the world will end, this is the way the world will end, this is the way the world will end, not with a bang, but a whimper."

He was wrong. This world is not going to end with a bang and it's not going to end with a whimper. The good news about the way the world will end is that the kingdoms of this world will become the kingdom of our God, and He shall reign forever and ever. Hallelujah!

The truth of the matter is that we are on the verge of

conquering the world for Jesus, and I'm inviting you to become witnesses, to become persons who influence people everywhere you go to join God's revolution. I'm inviting you to allow Jesus to make you into somebody who will go into every corner of the world, especially to those places where you are most desperately needed. I am calling you to go where you will make a world of difference in a world that yearns to be different. I'm asking you to let Jesus use you to begin to change His world.

You've probably heard this line a dozen times before. Most of you have grown up hearing this stuff. But you haven't done anything about it. You haven't acted.

Sören Kierkegaard told about a make-believe country where only ducks lived. On Sunday morning all the ducks came into church, waddled down the aisle, waddled into their pews, and squatted. Then the duck minister came in, took his place behind the pulpit, opened the Duck Bible and read, "Ducks! You have wings, and with wings, you can fly like eagles. You can soar into the sky! Ducks! You have wings!" All the ducks yelled, "Amen!" and then they all waddled home.

Maybe you have heard everything I've said before, but you have never acted on it. Maybe you've understood the radical nature of the call to discipleship, but you have never done anything about it. Maybe you've known for a long time that being a Christian means joining God's revolution, but you've never been willing to make a commitment to His cause. You, like the ducks in Kierkegaard's story, have not acted on the message you have heard. Well, the time has come to act—to do—to join—to commit.

Jesus is here right now, and He is saying to you, "Give Me your life. Join My revolution. Participate in My great movement in history. For My sake, in response to what I've done for you—give Me your life to do My will."

A friend of mine was on a train traveling out of Victoria Station in London. Across from him in the compartment were two men in their early thirties. Twenty minutes out of the station, one of them had an epileptic seizure. Perhaps you know how frightening such a seizure can be. The man stiffened and fell heavily out of his seat. Immediately, his friend took off his own jacket, rolled it up, and put it behind his friend's head. He blotted the beads of perspiration from his brow with his handkerchief, talked to the stricken man in a quiet manner, and calmed him. When the seizure was over, he lifted his friend gently back into his seat.

Then he turned to my friend and said, "Mister, please forgive us. Sometimes this happens two or three times a day. My buddy and I were in Vietnam together, and we were both wounded. I had bullets in both my legs and he had one in his shoulder. The helicopter that was supposed to come for us never came to pick us up.

"My friend picked me up, mister, and he carried me for

three and one-half days out of that jungle. The Vietcong were sniping at us the whole way. He was in more agony than I was. I begged him to drop me and save himself, but he wouldn't let me go. He got me out of that jungle, mister. He saved my life. I don't know how he did it and I don't know why he did it.

"Four years ago, I found out that he had this condition, so I sold my house in New York, took what money I had, and came over here to take care of him." And then he looked at his friend and said, "You see, mister, after what he did for me, *there isn't anything I wouldn't do for him*."

I'm not going to give the big fanfare or drum roll here. There's no choir singing "Just as I Am." Nevertheless, I want to ask you something while you are reading these words. I ask you to say, "I want to commit my life to Christian service. I'm ready to become a revolutionary for Jesus. I am not just going to believe in Jesus; I am going to surrender to Him without any reservations. God can use me to do anything He wants, anywhere He wants. I'll go wherever and say whatever and do whatever He leads. I am His without reservation, and if this means the mission field, I'm ready to go."

Sometimes when I raise this challenge at youth rallies, I see dozens of hands raised high. And I say, "My God, are you serious? I mean, are you *really* serious? Are there really this many kids ready to say, 'I'm ready to go anywhere, do anything'?" If all of you are serious, the revolution is about to explode!

DATING

TURNING YOUR LOVE LIFE OVER TO JESUS

Let's talk about young people's favorite topic, dating—not simply because it is something that every kid wants to discuss and think about, but because dating will exercise a decisive influence on how you carry out your Christian commitment. You know, and I know, that there are few things more important to young people between the ages of sixteen and twenty-four than dating. If you are going to be a Christian, it is important that you date right. It is important that you behave right on dates. It is important that you marry right. You blow your dating life, and you are likely to mess up your Christian commitment. I know of more kids who had fantastic promise for Christian service who blew it because they didn't date right.

I started dating when I was a senior in high school. That was a little late compared to other guys my age. And as I started dating, I was amazed to discover how much it cost. Dating is wildly expensive. I took this one girl out four times and I spent a total of $24.32 on her. Girls always laugh and say "cheapskate" when I admit that I was keeping track of how much I spent. But you guys know what I'm talking about. Of course guys keep track, because money spent on a girl while dating is an investment. If you spend a lot of money on them, they are obligated to you, right?

Now, girls, if you don't like the idea that you become obligated when a guy spends a lot of money on you, then perhaps you ought to take a note or two from the pages of the feminist handbook and not let him spend that much money on you. If you don't want to be manipulated into a stage of obligation to a guy, you should consider going "dutch."

One day I came into the lunchroom at West Philadelphia High, and there was my girl—my $24.32 girl—sitting there talking to another guy. And she wasn't just small-talking, she was serious-talking. I went over to the guy sitting next to her and said, "You ought to leave, see." In today's language, I would say something like "Take a hike" or "Get lost." The guy disappeared in a hurry.

My girl looked at me with a steel-like look and said, "Tony, four dates with you and you act like you own me." I said, "Agnes (I can't help it, that was her name!), for $24.32, I bought you!"

I know that was a terrible thing to say, but I really felt I had a claim on her. The girls reading this book probably are saying to themselves, "You know, that's what's the matter with guys. They go out with you a few times and spend a few bucks on you and they act like they own you."

This is just one of the things that is wrong with our dating system. Dating is too expensive and because of the expense, guys tend to want a commitment. I wanted a committed relationship as soon as I started dating because I, like you, know the following to be true: you spend the most money on a girl during the early stages of dating. Once you're committed, it's different. When kids date exclusively they mostly hang around the house (usually the girl's house) and drink Cokes (usually bought by her parents). And when things get boring, they make out.

The cost leads people to be manipulated into a commitment and it definitely leaves the females with a sense of being obligated to the guys. This often results in girls doing things with guys that they really would rather not do. At the very least, an expensive date requires an obligatory goodnight kiss from the girl. I worry about the Christian implications of this way of doing things. Does the Lord really want you to allow yourself to be maneuvered into a position where you have to deliver certain signs of affection that you neither mean nor intend?

But there is another thing wrong with the dating system, which from a Christian perspective is far more serious, and that is the value system implied in the American dating system. The system tends to get young people to put a premium on personal traits and characteristics that, in the long range of life, prove to be superficial. On the contrary, a number of things that really count in personal relationships are ignored. The kids who make it in the dating system are usually good-looking but may be shallow, while many quality people who aren't so good-looking don't stand a chance.

I never really saw the horror of all of this until my senior year at West Philadelphia High when I was elected student government president. That was a real ego trip. Being president of a student body of 4,500 students had me feeling like somebody special.

Then I realized that one of the things that went with the job was this: I was responsible for setting up and running the dances the school had each month. The trouble was that I belonged to one of those churches that didn't approve of dancing. Many a time our preacher would pound his pulpit and tell us, "Dancing stimulates the lust of the flesh!" Every time he laid that on us, I would start to fantasize and mumble to myself, "Yeah!" Of course, I have to say that he was probably right. If a couple of teenagers can gyrate face to face for three hours and not get turned on, they are not spiritual—they are dead! I think there is a naiveté about our thinking if we think that it is possible to dance suggestively without getting turned on. When kids get into that kind of dancing too heavily, they should not be surprised if their erotic feelings get out of hand.

Of course, fundamental churches like the one I went to back then can often be hypocritical. My church did not approve of dancing (because it stimulated the lust of the flesh), but our church did have hayrides. Undoubtedly you have been on a church hayride. If so, you know that there is always some guy with a guitar in the front of the wagon playing "Do Lord" while everybody else is in the straw "doing it." It's amazing to see how we evangelical Christians can be so blind to the consequences of what we do, while we self-righteously knock what others do.

Since our church didn't have dances and I was against dances, I told my high-school principal how I felt. He said, "You've got to do it, Tony. It is one of the responsibilities of the student body president." I finally gave in and on the appointed night did my job and set up for the dance. I had decided I would go but would not dance. I would be what sociologists call an "observer participant." I would appear to be a participant in the dance, but really would not get involved. So that night I was with the other kids and yet I was an outsider, observing what was going on with a clarity that somebody who was actually dancing could not have. What I saw was incredible.

Along with the decorating committee, I got to school about 6:30 to set up for the dance. We got the old crepe paper out and strung it diagonally across the gym. We set up folding chairs against the walls. Then we opened the windows of the gym because the basketball team had just finished practicing, and nobody likes to dance in the smell of a giant armpit.

After we had aired out the place, at about a quarter to seven, this kid named Roger (that's not his real name) showed up. Frankly, Roger was a loser. I mean, this kid was a disaster on wheels. I wondered as he walked in, "Why has Roger come? Nobody is going to want to dance with him. Most of the girls don't even like talking to him. Why is he here?"

But Roger did not come to dance. He had brought a stack of records and he was counting on being the disc jockey. He went up on the platform in the back of the gym where there was a record player and he played the records while the other kids danced. He played disc jockey all night. This was Roger's way of participating without getting hurt. He knew that if he ever stopped playing the records, came down from the platform, and asked some girl to dance, he would probably be rejected. Playing records was Roger's way of being involved in the dance without getting hurt.

I still remember the teacher who was chaperoning the

dance coming up to me at intermission and saying, "Hey, Tony, this is a wonderful dance! Everybody is having such a good time." And I looked at Roger and I wondered whether he was having a good time. I think not. I think Roger was hurting, hurting bad.

He wasn't the only one either. Sitting around the gym on the folding chairs were about forty girls, all sitting there with bored looks of indifference on their faces. You know the looks, looks that say, "Oh, wow, when is this dull night going to end?" But you know what those faces are concealing, don't you? When a girl is rejected, she puts on an air that she doesn't care. She pretends that she is bored with the whole scene, while down deep inside she is experiencing awful, awesome pain. As those girls sat there, I stood to the side and watched them hurting for half the evening because no one asked them to dance.

When the dance was over, I was out on Forty-eighth Street, joking and talking with some of my friends, when out of the gym came my science lab partner, Mary. Mary was a neat, neat girl; witty, humorous and, on top of that, she had mastered the art of ventriloquism. It is a very dangerous thing to sit next to a witty ventriloquist in chemistry class.

For instance, one day the teacher said, "We're going to have a test tomorrow." I raised my hand and asked, "What will it cover?" He said, "Oh, whatever is on my mind." Without moving her lips, Mary said in a husky voice, "Then we don't have anything to worry about." Everybody laughed and Mary looked at me as if to say, "How could you say something like that, Tony?"

Mary was a terrific person, but she did not have the greatest build in the world. She didn't have good-looking legs either. Our dating system is vicious to people who aren't shaped just right. That night Mary had been one of those girls who had spent the entire evening waiting, without luck, for someone to pay attention to her.

As she came out of the dance, Mary ran right by me. I tried to say, "Hi!" but she didn't answer. She got into her father's waiting car and before he could pull away from the curb, I watched her break down and start to cry.

I was furious. I was irate. I went into the principal's office the next day and said, "No more for me. I'm finished with dances." And he said, "You can't allow your religion to come between you and your responsibilities." I said, "Hey, my minister really didn't understand what's wrong with dancing. He only saw the sexual thing. What I saw last night was cruelty. I saw some of my best friends and some of the neatest kids in our school getting hurt."

Ask yourself this very simple question: "How many high-school kids do I know who are hurting because nobody ever asks them out on a date?" You can find kids in any American school every day who are hurting. And if you're going to act like a Christian, you will identify with those who hurt. You will feel their pain and their agony. I never went to another high-school dance. Not because I think dancing is wrong, but for another reason: I didn't want to be a part of a system that hurt innocent kids.

Incidentally, I get a little uptight with some churches that run banquets the night of the senior prom. They might not be promoting dancing, but it all boils down to the same thing if a young person needs a date to be part of the fun. Whenever you create a system for teenagers that requires them to have partners of the opposite sex in order to participate, then you've created a social system or activity that automatically excludes a lot of kids. Furthermore, you end up excluding those who most need to be included. You close out those who are hurting the most. As Christians, we should be reaching out to the persons whom society rejects. Instead, we sometimes unconsciously support a system that fosters their sense of rejection.

Jesus was committed to affirming those who were rejected by society. His life was an array of episodes in which He picked up people who were hurting and made them feel loved and significant. Jesus didn't exactly choose the most popular and attractive people to initiate His involvement. He said, "From the stones the builder rejects will come the stones out of which I will build My new world."

Here is the real issue: we have a dating system that glorifies the kids who are already glorified by our society and puts down the kids who are already put down. I feel bad for all the Marys of the world. I think Christians should be agonizing over what the American dating system is doing to people.

I know some people are going to say that I'm overstating the case. They will argue that the American dating system does not hurt kids. To such people I can only respond that you don't have to be a sociologist to see the hurts this system causes. Simple, honest observation will make this case.

A few years ago Janice Ian sold a million copies of a song. It was popular because it communicated the feelings of so many kids in America. Hurting teenagers listened intently whenever the song was played and thought to themselves, "That's me. That song is about me." The song goes like this:

I learned the truth at 17,
That love was meant for beauty queens
And high-school girls with clear-skin smiles.
While those of us with ravaged faces
Lacking in the social graces,
Desperately remained at home
Inventing lovers on the phone
Who called to say, "Come dance with me,"
And murmured vague obscenities.
It isn't all it seems, at 17,
For those of us who knew the pain

Of Valentines that never came
And those whose names were never called
When choosing sides for basketball,
It was long ago and far away.
The world was younger than today,
And chains were all they gave for free
To ugly-duckling girls like me, at 17.

The song tells it like it is and we Christians should be aware of that. The American dating system is making kids hurt. If you go to a school with a thousand kids, the system usually works for only about two hundred of them. Only two hundred out of a thousand get the praise, the strokes, and the recognition needed for a positive self-image. What about the other eight hundred who live their lives in "quiet desperation"? Shouldn't Christians be heartbroken over them?

I know attractive, personable girls who graduate from high school never having had a date, and those dateless years so devastate their sense of self-worth that they find themselves saying things like: "I'm nothing. Nobody could love me." The consequences of such self-contempt can destroy a girl's moral standards. Show me a girl with a lousy self-image and I'll show you a female who is very easy to sexually seduce. The female without a good self-concept is very easy to hustle because she doesn't feel like she's worth anything. And when a girl begins to feel that she is junk, she begins to act like junk. A girl's self-concept has a powerful effect on her actions. If she thinks she's trash, she'll act like trash. On the contrary, if she thinks she's a precious child of God, she will act like one. We must do our utmost to ensure that girls have the latter experience.

The time has come for Christians to look for alternatives to our present dating system. Christians ought to invent and promote a new style of dating.

When I was teaching at the University of Pennsylvania, I became intrigued with a new style of dating that was emerging on the campus scene during the 1960s. They called it "group dating." Instead of boys and girls going off as pairs, a whole gang of kids would run around together. Instead of going to a movie or a ball game with a date, about seven or eight fellows and girls would go together. Nobody worried about who was linked with whom. All the kids simply had a good time together and enjoyed each other.

I think your youth group, or Sunday school class, at church could do just that. Your Sunday school class could be more than just a gathering on Sunday night before church. It could be more than a mini church service for young people. Your church peers could become a gang of friends who provide a social life for each other. Your church peers could turn into a fellowship of people who have fun with each other every Friday and Saturday night. It doesn't take much for something wonderful like that to happen to a church group. All it takes is for somebody to speak for the group and say, "Hey! Come on with us and have some fun. We're not practicing exclusive dating. Everybody can come along with us. We want everybody to share. Let's have a good time together. It won't be as much fun without you." You'll be surprised at the response to that kind of invitation.

I wish that you would make the following commitment: "I am no longer going in for exclusive dating. I am going to foster group dating. It is all right for me to have a boyfriend or a girlfriend. But in social activities, I am going to make sure that everybody is invited, that everybody gets brought along, and that everybody participates. That's because it is a Christian obligation to reach out to the kids who feel left out and make them feel like they are included."

Spirituality is caring about people who are left out, caring about people who are hurting. If you get so consumed in your own dating that you forget about all of the kids who are left out, you are not behaving like a Christian.

We can't talk about dating without talking about sex. You knew I'd get to that eventually, didn't you? Here are some statistics: according to one study, 75 percent of all girls become sexually active by age nineteen. That means they have had sexual intercourse. The number of males who are sexually active by age nineteen is even higher at 85 percent ("Teen Sex and

Pregnancy," The Alan Guttmacher Institute, March 1999, www.agi-usa.org). Statistics like these are mind-boggling to those of us who grew up a generation ago. As you might expect, the statistics for Christian young people who have had sexual relations are somewhat lower, though not as low as you might think.

Some of you will ask with surprise, "You aren't talking about born-again, Bible-believing Christians, are you?" As a sociologist who is also an evangelical Christian, I've made a special study of our evangelical, Bible-believing kids, and my studies show that that's just about where they fall—or fail. It seems that we are living in an age in which even people who consider themselves followers of Jesus Christ have become pretty loose, sexually speaking.

That is frightening for a variety of reasons. First of all, if you are a Christian, you have to be aware of the fact that Jesus Christ is in you every minute of every day. You know what that means, don't you? It means that whenever you mess around, Jesus is involved in it with you. You can't leave Him outside the room when you mess around. You can't put Him out of your life temporarily because you want to do some things which you know will displease Him. When you are a Christian, He possesses you and involves Himself with all that you do. And so, when you do something degrading, or cheapen your-self in any way and then say, "The only person affected by

these actions of mine is me; I'm not hurting anybody else"—
you are only kidding yourself. If Jesus is in you, then what you
do not only affects you, it affects Jesus too. Makes sense,
doesn't it? Try reading 1 Corinthians 6:15–17.

Second, Jesus is also in the other person. The person you
might choose to use for your sexual games is also the temple of
the Lord. There are a host of unexplored implications in the
sayings of Jesus in Matthew 25:40, which reminds us that
whatever we do to another person, we are doing to Jesus.
Always realize that Jesus Christ is in you and that Jesus is in
the other person at the same time. In any and all relations with
others, Jesus is involved.

There is one last thing about sexual behavior. The Bible
says that we crucify Him anew each time we behave in a way
that is contrary to His will. Sin is not simply breaking the law
of God, it is re-crucifying Jesus. And that is meant to be taken
literally.

One of my students once said to me, "Look, I know I am
sleeping around and I know it is wrong. But after all, I really
believe that all of my sins were taken care of two thousand
years ago on the cross. I live under the grace of God." Believe
it or not, that's really what he told me. He did what he did
knowing it was wrong but claiming that his sins were atoned
for back then and there on Calvary's cross. He did not grasp
the fact that every time he bedded down with a pickup, he

crucified Jesus again. I wish that when that guy was doing his thing in bed he could hear the agonizing screams of Jesus. I wish he could hear Jesus crying and wailing. I wish he could experience what Jesus was going through at that very moment of what he was doing.

The Bible says, "Do not sin that grace may abound." Paul says, "Recognize that you crucify Jesus daily." Daily! So what am I saying? I'm saying this: if you are doing something that is obscene and if you are cheapening both yourself and your partner, you should also remember that at that very moment you are driving another nail into the hand of Jesus. You are once again lancing His side with a spear.

I am not saying that sex is obscene and dirty. Furthermore, I agree with the Freudian psychologists who claim that Victorian versions of Christianity have created unhealthy attitudes toward sexuality. Contrary to the Victorians, I am claiming that God has designed us for sexual enjoyment and that the gospel is good news for those who want to know how to maximize their sexual pleasures. The Bible outlines how this maximum gratification can be achieved: allow sex to express love within the context of a binding relationship (i.e., marriage). The sexual act is not dirty, but it becomes dirty if it is carried out in a way that is contrary to what is prescribed by our Lord. When sex enhances a love relationship, it is explosively wonderful.

Let me take a moment here to tell you about a way of messing around sexually that seems to be more common to Christians than to people who do not share Christian commandments. Christians, as I have said, are less likely to enter into sexual intercourse than non-Christians. However, while Christians may be less inclined to lose their virginity, they are the people who are most inclined to become what Alfred Kinsey, the great American sex researcher, called "*technical* virgins." By "technical virgin," Kinsey means a person who doesn't engage in sexual intercourse, but who does everything else. There are Christian young people who play with each other's sexual organs, make out in the nude, and mutually masturbate but do not "go all the way." In the midst of such circumstances, they try to kid themselves into believing that they are living within "Christian limits" for sexual behavior and are still "saving themselves sexually" until marriage.

We don't often talk about petting in Christian circles. But there is an awful lot of "very heavy sexual stuff" that goes on among Christian young people. It often gets so heavy that it diminishes their capability for spirituality and lessens their humanity. And even while such things are happening, they demonstrate a "technical self-righteousness" and applaud themselves because they haven't "gone all the way."

The reason I am going to such lengths in talking about sexual behavior among young people is that I know all too well how sexual behavior influences their thinking and belief systems. When I first came to teach at Eastern College, I was asked to be the chaplain for the school. Kids often would come to my office, sit down and tell me that they had stopped believing in Jesus Christ. And I almost always knew why. They had stopped believing in Jesus because they had been compromising their sex lives. They would invariably say, "Doctor, I no longer believe in Jesus because intellectually I find that the Christian faith is untenable." I always used to say, "And that is a lot of hogwash. Before we go any further in this discussion I want to ask you some questions about your sex life."

I know enough about the Christian faith and enough about the arenas of academia to know that there is nothing intellectual that cannot ultimately be reconciled with the Christian faith. Christianity and valid intellectual insights can be put together and harmonized if one has the will to do so. I know that the reason most students become skeptical and give up their faith is usually unrelated to the academic process. As Blaise Pascal, the brilliant French intellectual of the sixteenth century, once said, "Doubt comes from disobedience." If a Christian person is behaving sexually in a way that he or she knows is contrary to the will of God, that behavior creates cognitive dissonance. Good phrase, "cognitive dissonance." It means that there will be great inner tension when what a person does and tries to justify to the self is contrary to his or her established convictions.

There are two ways of resolving that guilt. Number one: a person can repent of the behavior that he/she knows is contrary to his/her spiritual convictions and thus reestablish a sense of inner well-being. The other way to eliminate the cognitive dissonance and feel good again is for the person to reject the convictions that condemn his/her behavior. To put it another way, a young person can get over guilt feelings if that person can put God out of his or her mind. If the person gets rid of God, then he/she can do anything without feeling guilt—or cognitive dissonance. The person doesn't feel condemned once God has been put out of his or her life because there is no longer the awareness of One who will negatively judge sexual exploitation or any other kind of sin.

Most religious skepticism and loss of spirituality results, not through intellectual processes, but from disobeying what is known to be the will of God, particularly in sexual matters. I know more kids who have had their faith destroyed through their sexual behavior than by anything else. That is one reason why I plead with you so strongly to be faithful to Jesus in sexual matters and to recognize what is going on in your head when you mess around with your body.

Having said all of this, I now want to talk about love. I know I've been talking a great deal about sex, but I want to turn our attention now to love.

I grew up on what this culture calls "romantic love." The

pop songs back then created my perspective on love. The pop songs in my day were different from those of today. In my day, you understood the words (I'm sure you've heard that line from your parents). One of the most popular love songs when I was a kid went like this: "Some enchanted evening, you will meet a stranger across a crowded room. And somehow you'll *know*." So I grew up looking across crowded rooms. Romance was my thing. I believed what the songs said and was sure that one day I would meet somebody who would overwhelm me with a single glance.

Romance *does* happen. Instantaneous "turnons" do occur. But love is deeper than romance. Romance is an on-again, off-again feeling. You know that. You probably have had several very intense romantic turnons by this stage of your life. While each of them was delicious at the time and while you swore to yourself it would last forever, you must admit that it didn't last. It ended, and later on you had another turnon with somebody else. Come on! Be honest! Isn't it true that two years ago you were head over heels in a romantic affair that you were sure would never end—and it did?

Whereas romance simply "happens" and is an on-again, off-again affair, love must be created and it has a constancy about it. As the Bible says, "Love never fails" (1 Cor. 13:8). When I got married forty-five years ago, I was very romantic, but I'm not sure I was a very loving husband. My wife will verify that I am much more loving today than I was on our wedding day, even though I may be somewhat less romantic.

One night we were coming home from New Jersey, zipping across Walt Whitman Bridge into Philadelphia, and my wife said, "Look at us! *Look at us!*"

"What's the matter?" I asked.

She said, "Look where you're sitting."

I said, "I am driving the car. When you are driving the car, it is best to sit behind the wheel."

"Look at them!" she said. "Look at them!"

So I looked into the car in front of us and there was this guy who looked like he had two heads. (You know what I mean, don't you?)

We crossed the bridge into Philly and all the while I was aware that my wife was all upset because we weren't as romantic as we once had been. As we drove through the city we traveled through Fairmount Park. I noticed a parking place for "make outs." It was located right on the riverbank. It was perfect. I stopped the car, switched off the ignition, turned on the parking lights (fortunately the kids were still asleep in the backseat), reached out and grabbed my wife, pulled her over (and smashed her head on the steering wheel). And she said, "What are you doing?"

I said, "I'm being romantic."

She said, "Take me home."

So much for being romantic. Romance is nice stuff, and it does happen. It happens often but it should not be trusted. I must admit that I often have romantic turnons but I try not to take them seriously. You're thinking, "Campolo, you're an old man of sixty-eight. You're bald. You ought to be beyond all that sort of thing." Not at all. The old motor's still running. I often have romantic fantasies. I'm not proud of that fact. But such things do happen to me. Yes! Even at my age.

You are naive if you think that once you accept Jesus you are not going to experience these kinds of emotional reactions anymore. If you believe that, you are going to be very vulnerable to Satan, because nobody is in a more precarious position than the individual who thinks he or she is spiritually safe and secure. The person who believes that he or she can't be seduced is the one who is most likely to get blown away.

What Christians should recognize is that there is a deeper kind of love than romance. The ancient Greeks called it *philos*. It's the kind of love that grows up between two people who have the same goals and commitments in life. It's a love that grows up between two people who are working toward something they both hold dear. This is the kind of love Christians should create in their relationships. This kind of love goes much deeper than romance.

Imagine a triangle. Along the base of the triangle are all the things that you say are important to you. As you move toward the apex of the triangle, the base will get smaller and smaller, leaving room for fewer and fewer things. Eventually, there is room for only one thing. Then you have to answer this question: "What is that one thing that you will hold on to after you have sacrificed everything else?" What is your ultimate concern? What is that for which you would die?

Once you have defined what is so important to you that you are willing to sacrifice everything else to hold on to it, you ought to look for somebody else who has the same commitment.

If you are a Christian, by definition you are somebody who is committed to Jesus; you are someone who says from the depths of your being, "For me to live is Christ, to die is gain." You are ready to live for Jesus 100 percent. Consequently, if you are a Christian, and you want to experience this deeper kind of love called *philos*, you must marry someone who shares your commitment to Jesus. As each of you grows closer to Jesus, you will simultaneously grow closer and closer to each other. That is why the Bible tells us, "Be ye not unequally yoked with nonbelievers" (2 Cor. 6:14). In the Old Testament, the Bible asks, "Can two walk together, except they be agreed?" (Amos 3:3). For a love relationship to work over the long haul, it is essential for you and your partner to agree on a purpose for life. It is essential that you both believe the same things about Christ.

All too seldom when kids are dating do they carry on philosophical discussions. You're thinking, "Philosophical discussions, you've got to be kidding! Where are you at, Tony baby?" Hey, the most important thing you can do with your partner is to find out where that other person is coming from and where he or she is going. Be sure to discuss your commitments together. If the two of you are not committed to the same things, you will not be able to develop a commitment to each other.

I remember so well a certain young woman at Eastern College who had committed herself to be a missionary with Wycliffe Bible Translators. She had been dating a guy named John and one day she came into my office with tears running down her cheeks. She sat down and buried her head in her hands. With concern and perplexity, I asked, "What's the matter?"

She said, "John wants to marry me."

"You like him, don't you?" I asked.

She said, "I'm crazy about John."

"Well, then, what's the problem? You love John. John wants to marry you. Sounds perfect."

"John is not committed to Jesus," she answered. "He doesn't share my commitment to go as a missionary to Brazil."

"What are you gong to do?" I asked.

Her eyes narrowed as she looked at me and said, "You know

what I'm going to do. I'm going to Brazil as a missionary. I just came in here for you to pray with me—and cry with me."

And I did both.

One Friday afternoon John and I got into a car, drove that young woman to Kennedy Airport in New York, and put her on a plane to fly to Brazil. When she boarded that plane, she was crying, John was crying, and I was crying. And as she flew away, I thought to myself, "Is this what it means to be a follower of Christ? Is this what it means to be a disciple of our Lord?" And the answer is, "You bet your life."

Jesus says, "Unless you love me more than you love your mother, your father, your sister, or your brother, you are not worthy of me." (Matt. 10:37 NIV). You can't be a follower of Jesus unless you are into that. I can give you another case in which the result of a love relationship was a rejection of the Lord's will. A couple came to me to be married. I knew the young woman well. She had made a commitment to Christ in a Bible study group I had led. Her fiancé was a complete stranger to me. When I asked him if he was a Christian, he coolly announced that he had once believed in God but had "grown out of that sort of thing."

I asked the young woman if she was going to marry him in spite of the fact that he wasn't a Christian. She angrily replied, "Don't go quoting the Bible to me, Campolo. You're always quoting the Bible." I don't know what she thought I was going to quote. Shakespeare? She went on, "You're probably going to quote that verse, 'Be not unequally yoked to nonbelievers,' aren't you? Don't you understand? I love him, and nothing is going to stand in the way of our being together."

I told her that she could not be a true Christian unless she loved Jesus more than she loved her fiancé, but she would not listen. However, something did get in the way of the two of them being together for the rest of their lives. They got divorced. I don't think a marriage can work if it's built upon the necessity of going against the known will of God.

Christian lovers are people who know there is a kind of love different from the romance that this society calls love. Christian lovers know there is a kind of love that comes into their lives, possesses them, and allows Jesus to flow through them into the lives of the other person. In such a relationship, each Christian lover knows that Jesus wants to love the other person through him or her. I call upon you to be Christian lovers.

There is a children's story that I have loved for a long time, and it still moves me every time I read it. It is called *The Velveteen Rabbit*, and was written by Margery Williams. In one passage, a toy rabbit and a toy horse are talking to each other. Their conversation, which I believe communicates a great deal of truth, goes like this:

"What is Real?" asked the Rabbit one day, as they were lying side by side near the nursery fender, just before Nan came in to tidy up the room. "Does it mean having things that buzz inside you and a stick-out handle?"

"Real isn't how you are made," said the Skin Horse. "It's a thing that happens to you. When a child loves you for a long, long time, not just to play with, but *really* loves you, then you become Real."

"Does it hurt?" asked the Rabbit.

"Sometimes," said the Skin Horse, for he was always truthful. "When you are Real, you don't mind being hurt."

"Does it happen all at once, like being wound up," he asked, "or bit by bit?"

"It doesn't happen all at once," said the Skin Horse.

"You become. It takes a long time. That's why it doesn't often happen to people who break easily, or have sharp edges, or who have to be carefully kept. Generally, by the time you are Real, most of your hair has been loved off, and your eyes drop out and you get loose in the joints and very shabby. But these things don't matter at all, because once you are Real, you can't be ugly except to people who don't understand."

What I have described to you is so much deeper than romance, and this is what Jesus wants for you. He wants you to have a relationship in which you and your partner become more alive, more real, more vital. When you have that kind of relationship, it creates a sense of excitement, a sense of euphoria, an unspeakable joy. When you are turned on to somebody who shares the same commitment that you do, then you are in love with somebody who is in love with the same Jesus that you love. When both you and your partner can say, "We are going to serve Jesus Christ together," you will have an explosive excitement that will make your life together all that you hoped it would be.

One last thing: in most dating relationships, there are times when you feel like breaking up and there may come a time when you do have to break up. If that time comes in your dating relationship, please, please handle it with honesty. I find that a lot of Christian kids refuse to be honest in such situations.

Too often when a girl wants to break up with a guy, she doesn't just tell him. Instead she thinks that it is better to make life miserable for him. She figures that if she hurts him enough, he will break up with her and then she won't have to do the dirty work. Of course it happens the other way around, as well. There are guys who utilize the same strategy when they break up with girls.

I have seen kids hurt each other so much in the process of breaking up that after their romantic relationship is over, they can't even be friends anymore. You see that all around you in school every day, don't you? You know kids who used to be "in love" but who don't even speak anymore. The Bible teaches, "Be ye kind one to another, tenderhearted, forgiving one another, even as God for Christ's sake hath forgiven you" (Eph. 4:32). Are you kind to the people you date?

I'm old enough to remember Elvis Presley singing, "Don't Be Cruel." There is so much cruelty among young people in today's world. And I have seen too many Christian young people who are cruel in the ways that they end romantic relationships. I call you to be kind and honest in the process of breaking up.

Some of you reading this book will have to face the possibility of remaining single. There will be a significant number of you who will not get married. Perhaps you may find yourself in a place where you either have to choose between marrying somebody who doesn't believe in what you believe in and doesn't share your commitments, or not getting married at all. That is a hard choice to face, but I must tell you that there are a lot of things worse than being single the rest of your life. One of those is being married to someone with whom you do not have a camaraderie in the things of God.

I ask you to recognize that you may be asked to accept singleness if you follow Jesus. But nobody ever said that following Jesus would be easy. On the other hand, singleness can be a blessing. It can allow a person to serve Jesus in a way that is impossible for married people. The apostle Paul writes in 1 Corinthians 7:32–34:

> I would like you to be free from concern. An unmarried man is concerned about the Lord's affairs—how he can please the Lord. But a married man is concerned about the affairs of this world—how he can please his wife—and his interests are divided. An unmarried woman or virgin is concerned about the Lord's affairs: Her aim is to be devoted to the Lord in both body and spirit. But a married woman is concerned about the affairs of this world—how she can please her husband. (NIV)

Paul makes clear what anybody who has been to the mission field knows: the unencumbered state of single Christian workers makes them capable of doing things for Jesus that married people can never do. Single people can live in places where married people with children do not feel they should raise children. They are able to move from place to place as needs arise, with a minimum of difficulty. They require very little money for support. And they have more time to devote to those whom God has called them to serve. Singleness should not be viewed as a punishment to be endured, but as an opportunity for vast possibilities of service.

I am calling upon you to surrender your life to Jesus. This requires that you order your dating life, sex life, marriage or state of singleness in accord with His will. If I were to ask you to give your money to Jesus, I have a feeling that you might do that. If I asked you to give some time to Jesus, most of you would do that too. But I am asking for something deeper than that. I'm asking you to say from the depths of your heart, "Jesus, I am going to let You govern my life with members of the opposite sex. I am going to behave on dates in a way that will meet Your approval. I am going to be sensitive to the kids who are hurting and left out. I am going to commit myself only to people who share my commitments to You, because I know that You want me to have a love relationship that will make me real. I will accept singleness as an opportunity for greater service if You give me the special grace to overcome my sexual longings."

Will you do it? Will you give your love life over to Jesus and trust Him that His way of doing things is the best way? I sure hope so. More than that, I pray so.

DISCIPLESHIP

LIVING LIFE TO THE NTH DEGREE

In this chapter I'm going to talk to you about how to stay a Christian. The problem I'm dealing with is maintenance. Studies indicate that most of the people who come down the aisle in revival meetings do not remain Christians. You know that many of the people who say they have made a commitment to Jesus fall by the wayside. I don't know what the theological implications of these realities might be, and I leave it to the theologians to fight over the responsibilities of whether or not one can stop being a Christian. But I do know that Jesus made clear that not all those who receive His Word become fruitful servants of God. Read Matthew 13 if you want proof of what I say. In my experience, a survey of people who have made public commitments to Jesus would reveal that many of them, ten years later, have little to do with the church or the Christian lifestyle. There is a tremendous loss of people who make decisions for Jesus Christ, but who do not follow through.

Whenever I address young people and have them respond to my invitation to follow Jesus, I usually experience a strange kind of depression. The depression results from the fact that I know that a significant proportion of them will not be walking with Jesus ten years later. And the reason they will not be walking with Jesus is that they will not have done the things I am going to suggest that you do in the next few pages. If new converts would follow these suggestions, I could almost guarantee that they would be in step with Christ for the rest of their lives. I hope that you will give careful attention to these biblically prescribed instructions that I believe to be essential for the maintenance of the Christian life.

The first thing in maintaining yourself as a Christian is to recognize that you've got to get into Bible study. You knew I was going to say that, didn't you? I know that when you read the Bible it sometimes gets pretty boring. You and I may as well admit that right now. However, one reason Bible reading might seem boring could be that you read it improperly.

My mistake when I began to read the Bible was that I

started in Genesis and tried to read the whole Bible through from the beginning to the end. Genesis was okay, but when I got to Leviticus and everybody was "begatting" somebody else in those incredible genealogies, that's when it really got to me. And that's when I tended to give up on the whole project. I would make promises, usually at summer camp, to read the Bible. I'd say, "God, I promise to read a chapter a day to keep the devil away," or something like that. But reading the Bible just never seemed to be an ongoing proposition with me. If I had gotten some decent instructions about *how* to go about daily Bible reading, it might have been different. That's why I am so eager to give some direction to you. Perhaps your Bible reading time will go better than mine did when I was your age.

The first thing about reading the Bible is that you've got to know Jesus. You have to have a personal relationship with Him. Only then will the Bible have the kind of excitement about it that will leave you wanting to read more of it.

When I went off to college, my mother gave me a book called *The Silver Trumpet*. It was written by a man named J. Wesley Ingles. I read it and I thought it was a pretty good book, but it didn't blow me away or do anything special to me. Then at the end of my first semester at college, I reread the book. The second time I read it, that book had an aliveness and a power to it that it lacked in the first reading. Why? What caused the change? The answer can be found in the fact that during my freshman year my English teacher had been J. Wesley Ingles, the author of that book. The man who had written it was my teacher and the fact that I knew the author made all the difference in the world when I read the book.

The reason the Bible doesn't come alive to many people is that they don't know the Author personally. If that's your problem, why not get to know the Author of the Bible right now? Jesus is there with you. He wants to become your personal friend. All you have to do is say within yourself as deeply as you know how, "Jesus, I want You to be my personal friend. I want You to come into my life. I want You to possess me."

Ask Him to come into your life and He will. The Bible says that He stands at the door of your heart and knocks. The Scriptures teach that if you'll just say, "Okay, come in and take possession of me," He will do it. He will come in and take possession of you. When that happens He will equip you to understand the Scriptures in a way that otherwise would have been impossible. The Holy Spirit, who is Jesus spiritually present with you, interprets the Scripture for you as you read it. When you are under the Spirit's direction, the Bible's meaning for you will become clear and powerful. You can buy a thousand commentaries, you can go to a hundred Bible studies, but nothing will help you to understand what the Bible is saying more than the presence of the Holy Spirit in your life. This is the first thing you've got to know.

Second, you've got to have an orderly progression in your study of the Bible. Let me suggest that you begin by reading the Gospel of Mark. It would be great if you would say, "This year I am going to read the Gospel of Mark through twenty times." Why twenty times? Because I think that it is more important to know the Gospel of Mark backward and forward and inside out than just to read the Bible through superficially.

Every once in a while someone tells me proudly, "I just finished reading the Bible through from cover to cover." I feel like asking that person, "How much of it do you remember? Did it affect you while you were reading it? Did you savor and ponder its words or did you just read for the sake of reading it?"

I want you to know the Gospel of Mark so well that if somebody asks, "Hey! What does the Bible say about material wealth?" you can say, "Let me quote to you from the tenth chapter of Mark." And right away you'll be able to quote the relevant passage about the rich young ruler. I believe you ought to read Mark and read it and read it some more, and that you ought to memorize whole sections of it if you can.

Scholars tell us that Mark served as a kind of director of religious education among Christians in the early church. Paul would win people to Jesus and Barnabas would pastor them, but it was Mark's job to teach new converts that they needed to know about the life of Jesus. Some biblical scholars suggest that the first-century Christians were required—are you ready for this?—to memorize what is now the entire book of Mark. That was one of the ways in which they were discipled into the church.

The Gospel of Mark was written to provide a basis to help new Christians become acquainted with the most important elements of the life and teachings of Jesus. That is why I am suggesting it to you. The Gospel of Mark was good for young Christians in the first century, so it ought to be good for you if you are just starting out in your Christian walk. Read it through and learn it in depth.

After the book of Mark, I would suggest that you study the Epistle of James. Read James through ten, fifteen, or twenty times until you know it backward, forward, and inside out too. The book of James talks about very practical things that you really need to know. It covers topics like gossiping, how to use your money, how to treat people, and how to act toward your parents. All kinds of important things are outlined in James.

I hope that I've made it clear that the way to study the Bible is to go at it one book at a time. That has been my style and it has served me well. Right now I am really pushing through the Epistle to the Ephesians. That's my book for this year and I guarantee you that by the end of this year, I'm going to *know* the Epistle to the Ephesians. I hope you will adopt an "in-depth" style of Bible reading and abandon the kind of superficial reading that characterizes the Bible study of too many Christians.

The second thing you've got to get into is prayer. Here is something that too few of us do very well. It isn't enough to get into praying when we want something—like just before an exam at school. Many people get very spiritual when a test paper stares them in the face. Then they pray, "God, give me the answers. I know I never cracked a book; but Lord, You are able to transform things. You are able to transfer the knowledge from the book into my head and onto the paper. Please, Jesus, do it—that I might be faithful to You." But most of the time it doesn't work to pray when you haven't studied—at least it never worked for me.

Then some of you are like my son. When he was just a little tyke, he came into the living room one night and said, "I'm going to bed, and I'm going to be praying. Anybody want anything?" (I love it!) You act like prayer is a way of getting whatever you want, regardless of how self-centered your request might be. Too often we treat prayer as though it is a time when we can read off a list of nonnegotiable demands to the Almighty.

It is intriguing to note that the Bible says the Lord knows what we have need of before we even ask. For instance, when we say, "Dear Lord, Sister Mary is sick in the hospital," the Lord is not saying, "Oh, I didn't know that! Thanks for filling Me in, Tony."

God is God and He knows what you have need of before you ask. Now that statement may leave you wondering, "So why even ask?" I've often wondered about that myself. If God knows what we need before we ask, why do we even have to bother to ask? The answer is simple. We need to make our requests known to God, not because it is necessary to inform Him of our needs, but because we need to establish what theologians call "a relationship of dependency" with God. We need to tell God what we need, not because God is ignorant of our needs, but because we need to know that we are dependent upon Jesus for everything.

One of my non-Christian friends claims that he rejects Christianity because it makes people depend upon God when they should depend upon themselves. He claims that Christianity is a crutch for weak people and makes them less than self-sufficient. What my friend does not realize is how weak we humans really are. He is deceived if he thinks that we can solve the ultimate problems of our lives without being dependent upon God. We all need to lean on something. Frankly, I'm relieved, more than words can express, that Jesus says, "Come, lean on Me." Lean on the everlasting arms. That's what prayer is all about. It's taking time to lean on Jesus. It's acknowledging that without God we can do nothing.

When we come to God in prayer, He invites us to talk to Him in an intimate manner. There is a time and a place for the formal types of prayer that they teach ministers in seminaries, and which characterize church liturgies. And if a formal prayer is required, I know how to deliver one. Try this one, for example:

> Oh, Thou great Creator of the universe. Oh, Thou who doth provide us with every good and perfect gift. Oh, Thou who doth give us the sun in the morning and the stars at night. We beseech Thee to be present and bless us on this occasion.

I hope you're impressed.

On the other hand, consider this: when my son was twenty years old, I could not have imagined him walking into our house and saying to me, "Oh, thou chairman of the sociology department at Eastern College; oh, thou who doth clothe me, feed me, and provide me with every good and perfect gift; I beseech thee this day, lend me the car." That's not the way he talks to me. I'm his daddy. So, like a good Italian boy, he would walk into the house, throw his arms around me, kiss me, and say, "Hi, Dad. Can I borrow the car?" You see, we love each other.

Jesus wants each of us to be intimate with Him. That is why the apostle Paul tells us in the eighth chapter of Romans that we should not pray as people filled with fear, but we should talk to God as one who is closer than any father could ever be. Actually, the apostle Paul instructs us to address God as "Abba," which is the ancient Hebrew word for "daddy." There is no one who wants to be closer to you than Jesus does. He doesn't want to be regarded as some transcendental Shylock, demanding His pound of flesh. He wants to be intimate with you. Be sure to talk to Jesus with the intense love and intimacy which He desires from you.

There's one more thing I want to tell you about praying. And that is, when we pray we should allow God time to answer. Too often we pray and pray and pray, and we do all the talking. Then when we are finished talking, we end the prayer. We leave no time for God to speak to us.

Suppose I called you on the telephone and I said, "Glenn (or whatever your name is), how are you doing? I'm sure looking forward to being in town and seeing you. It's going to be nice being your guest. We are going to have a great time together, aren't we? See you then." Then, without giving you a chance to reply, I hung up, turned to my wife, and said, "Funny thing about Glenn. He's a nice guy, but he never speaks to me!" My wife would say, "Speak to you? You never gave him a chance to talk!"

Isn't that the way we treat God? We never give Him a chance to speak to us either. We talk, talk, talk, and after we finish telling God what He already knows, we hang up. Right? We say, "I ask these things in Jesus' name, amen." Period. Dial tone. It must be frustrating to be God. Just when He hopes that we will listen to Him—we hang up on Him.

The Bible says, "Be still, and know that I am God" (Ps. 46:10).

Another way of translating that—the "Authorized Tony Campolo Translation"—is, "Shut up! Knock it off and let Me speak to you!" Each of us must learn the art of being silent and letting God speak. It took me a long time before I was able to be inwardly still so that God would speak to me. But contrary to some opinions, God does speak to people. The problem is that most of us don't give Him a chance to speak. We think that God does not personally address us, when, in reality, we fail to take the steps to create the situation in which we can become sensitive to Him.

It takes me about fifteen to twenty minutes to get ready before God can speak to me, because it takes me that long to become still. Inwardly still. It takes me between fifteen and twenty minutes before all the noise that is running around in my mind dies down and I become inwardly quiet. Only then do I begin to experience inner stillness. Only when I am inwardly quiet do I begin to sense God speaking to me.

The Scriptures say that God doesn't have a voice that is loud like thunder. His voice is not like a roaring fire. The Bible says that when God speaks, it is in a still, soft voice. That implies that only those who are inwardly quiet can receive His messages. When I wait in silence, God does speak to me. His messages do not come in words, but in feelings. Like "the rumblings of deep water," I sense Him moving in the depths of my being. I can't tell you how many times I have gone to prayer confused and upset, and have found in the stillness a God who gives me a peace that passes all understanding. I can't begin to tell you how many times I have gone to prayer confused and frustrated and found in God a sense of direction, a sense of purpose, a sense of calm.

Prayer is incredibly essential. It is through prayer that one gets a sense of being led by God, a sense of being guided by God, and a sense of God's direction for life. The Bible says, "As many as are led by the Spirit of God, they are the sons of God" (Rom. 8:14). Through prayer, one gets that leading.

There are two ways that I can tell you how to get to my house near Philadelphia. I can draw you a map, give it to you and say, "Go ahead, follow this map." You may or may not get there.

The other thing I can do is to say, "Get in the car and I will come along with you. I will show you how to get from here to there. I will guide you every inch of the way. I will tell you where to turn and I will tell you what route to take. Instead of a map, I will give you my presence."

God does something like the latter. He doesn't provide a road map that lays out the path of your life from beginning to end. Instead, He says, "I'll go with you all the way. I'll direct you as we go along. I'll keep you on the way you should go. Through prayer, I will help you to sense the path I want you to follow."

Every once in a while some high-school or college student comes to me and says, "I want to discover the will of God for my life." Now I haven't the slightest idea how to do that. Nowhere in the Bible does it say that God is going to give you a plan of your entire life. He never said that He would lay out His plan for your life in CinemaScope so you can view it in its entirety. What He *does* promise is to lead you *as* you go; to direct you day by day; to show you His will hour by hour. If you are sensitive to Him, sensitive to His leading—and that is what prayer is all about—He promises to personally guide you every step of the way.

I assure you that I had no idea ten years ago that I would be doing what I am doing today. And I have no idea where God wants me to be ten years from now. But that doesn't upset me. I trust God and believe that He will take care of me. I feel like He's saying to me, "You will sense through prayer where I want to take you and you can rest assured that everything will turn out to be good for you." I can take Him at His word when He says, "If you are willing to listen to Me and to be led by My Spirit, you will be My child and I will abide with you forever."

At this point in our discussion, I want to talk to you about how to stay faithful in your commitment to grow spiritually. I want to share with you a very important lesson that I have learned about how to keep up my personal Bible study and maintain a personal prayer life. Until I learned this lesson, my Christian growth pattern was an on-again, off-again thing. After hearing some inspirational speaker or attending a Christian conference, I would be very devoted to Bible reading and prayer. But after a few weeks, I would slip away from a pattern of daily devotions and quiet time. As many times as I promised God that this would not happen, it would happen. I couldn't be trusted to maintain a faithful lifestyle. Then I learned this lesson: nobody can be trusted to maintain a life of dedication to a Christian lifestyle without the support of others. No one can remain committed without a support group. It took me a long time to realize that I needed some brothers in Christ to assume responsibility for my spiritual development.

Years ago I got together with three other guys and we formed a *support group*. These three friends meet with me on Thursday mornings and for a couple of hours we talk together, pray together, and joke with each other. We tell each other what is going on in our respective lives. We talk about our problems. We provide encouragement for each other and correct each other. It is this small group that turns me on and keeps me alive spiritually. Unless each of you gets into some kind of support group, I don't think you're going to make it as a Christian. I don't think you're going to be consistently faithful. I don't think you're going to stay alive spiritually.

The problem for most young people is that they all have had experiences in their lives when they have had intense spiritual "turnons." You remember them. Perhaps it was at some

Christian camp and the scene was like this: Everybody was sitting around the campfire having just sung a thousand verses of "Kum-Ba-Yah." The speaker, who had given the devotional messages all week long, was starting his last talk with the hope of getting the campers to make commitments to Christ. He probably said, "Kids, we've had a real good time this week, haven't we?" With that, everyone looks sweetly at each other.

"We've come to really care about each other too." People start holding hands.

Then he pulls this one: "You know, gang, this is probably the last time we'll ever be together like this." That does it. A hundred kids start crying simultaneously.

His next line is predictable. "Okay, gang, you are alive in Jesus now, but are you going to be alive a week from now? Two weeks from now? It is easy to be a Christian when you are up here on the mountaintop, but what about when you are back in your schools? What will you be like when you're down in the valley after this summer camp is over?"

In such a setting, you and most of the other kids around the campfire made decisions to follow Jesus. You made decisions to read the Bible daily and to pray. You were sure you would never lose the spiritual aliveness of that moment—but you did.

Or perhaps your commitment was made at a revival meeting at church. You went down the aisle when the preacher gave the invitation. You were taken from the sanctuary into a prayer room where a counselor prayed with you and you promised God that you would do those things essential for spiritual growth and development—but you failed to keep your promise.

There was once a man who could be counted upon to go down the aisle at revival meetings in order to recommit his life to Christ. Each time he would get down on his knees at the altar and yell, "Fill me, Jesus! Fill me, Jesus!" He'd get all psyched up with religion, but three weeks later he would lose his excitement and be right back in the same old worldly ways. Every time a new evangelist hit town and held meetings, the man would go through the same routine. He'd go down the aisle, get down on his knees at the altar, and shout over and over again, "Fill me, Jesus!" People became cynical about his commitments at the altar, and one time when he was doing his thing and yelling, "Fill me, Jesus! Fill me, Jesus!" some lady at the back of the church shouted, "Don't do it, Lord! He leaks!"

That is one of the great problems of the Christian life, isn't it? We leak. All of us have had some super-duper spiritual experience in which we felt close to God, but soon found out that it didn't last. All of us feel like we leak. We seem to lose our zeal and excitement. All of us fail to carry out faithfully the commitments we have made to do the will of God.

To make the situation more problematic, there's always

some joker who stupidly says, "Yeah, but if it had been a real experience with God in the first place, it would have lasted." Which naturally leads you to believe your experience wasn't real. Don't be deceived. Even a *real* spiritual experience will not last. We all lose it. We *all* leak.

Well, then, what's the answer? How does a person keep from leaking? The bad news is that we can't stop the leaking. The good news is that each of us can be refilled regularly. Being regularly refilled is what Jesus wants for us. He doesn't expect you and me to have some kind of superspiritual one-time fill-ing with His Spirit to carry us the rest of our lives. Instead, He wants us to be *constantly refilled* with the Holy Spirit. And that is why each of us must be a part of a small support group.

The primary function of a support group is to regularly provide spiritual renewal for its members. That's what my group does for me. They fill me, they enliven me. What they do for me with each weekly meeting is to bring me back to life. The world literally kills me. My spirit becomes deadened through my interactions with so many people I meet in my daily round of activities, but that group brings me back to life.

I know you've heard of the Holy Spirit. That same God who came down and lived in Jesus Christ two thousand years ago, is present with us today as One called the Holy Spirit. And as the Holy Spirit, God can become a powerful presence in our lives. However, many of us fail to realize that one of the best ways to become receptive to the infilling of the Holy Spirit is through the conditions created by the fellowship of a support group. The Scripture says, "Where two or three are gathered together in my name, there am I in the midst of them" (Matt. 18:20). The Bible is telling us that the Spirit of God becomes a dynamic presence when a support group gets together in the name of Jesus and seeks the spiritual renewal He promises to all who gather together in His name.

One morning I got together with the members of my group just before taking a trip to Chicago. It was one of those times when we were sharing and talking on a very deep level, and I felt the Spirit of God flow into me and enrich me. I felt alive and powerful as my friends renewed me spiritually. I knew I had been refilled with the Spirit when I left that meeting. I went to the Philadelphia airport to catch the plane to Chicago, still feeling a glowing sensation derived from my support group. When I got on the plane, I found myself next to a businessman who obviously was very upset. There are few things as scary as being on an airplane seated next to a nervous man. You always wonder whether he knows something you don't know.

I wanted to share Jesus with that poor guy, but I didn't know how to start the conversation. I wanted to tell him that Jesus could help him, but I didn't know how to go about it. Suddenly, I felt that the Lord was leading me to do something that you might think is peculiar. I focused my mind on that man. You can call it telepathy, you can call it ESP, you can call it anything you like, but I just mentally zapped him. I focused all of my spiritual power on him. I closed my eyes and mentally concentrated on him. Over and over I kept focusing the name of "Jesus" on him. Without saying a word, I tried to communicate the love of Jesus to that man. My support group had empowered me and I was giving the power derived from my group to this stranger. I sat there and bombarded that guy's mind with Jesus all the way to Chicago. I focused "Jesus" on him the whole trip.

When the plane touched down at O'Hare Field in Chicago, I prayed, "Lord, I have been sharing You with this guy for the last two hours. If You want me to talk to him, give me a sign." With that, my seatmate nudged me and said, "Mister, I've got problems and I want to talk to you. I think you can tell me about God." What is amazing is that I wasn't surprised. I *expected* him to make that move. After all, I had been focusing the Holy Spirit on him for two whole hours.

The two of us went into the airport terminal and over cups of hot chocolate, talked about spiritual things for a long time. When we were through, he accepted the Lord. He responded to the invitation to allow Jesus to become Lord of his life. I believe that he became a Christian because my support group had equipped me to minister to him in the power of the Holy

Spirit even when words were not being uttered. I believe that the power of the Holy Spirit derived from fellowship with my three friends empowered me to enable that man to experience the presence of Jesus in a very special way. I believe that my nonverbal communication with him made him ready for what I would say to him.

Too many times when we want to share Jesus with somebody, we try to do it with clever words. We think that if we've got the right words or the right technique, we can win people to the Lord. Some of us think that all we have to do is take some course and learn the correct approach to witnessing and people will respond to us. But if all we come with is a Bible verse or a memorized technique, we're going to fail. The Four Spiritual Laws are among the best tools for evangelism—but they're simply not enough. The apostle Paul once said, "My message and my preaching were not with wise and persuasive words, but with a demonstration of the Spirit's power" (1 Cor. 2:4 NIV). We too must learn that the good words are effective in evangelistic outreach only if they are undergirded with the Spirit of God.

The Bible says, "I am not ashamed of the gospel of Christ: for it is the *power* of God unto salvation" (Rom. 1:16). God wants to empower you, but there is a great likelihood that you are not going to have His power unless you belong to a little support group. This is the point that I am trying very hard to make: *Jesus empowers you through fellowship*. If you were reading this as part of a class assignment, I would make you write that down and underline it. *Jesus empowers you through fellowship*.

I want you to form a support group with two or three of your friends. Choose people whose company you enjoy and with whom you have a lot in common. Ask these people if they would be willing to enter into a covenant with you. The members of this group must be willing to care for one another and assume responsibility for one another in spiritual matters.

Jesus had such a group, didn't He? You can name them. His little support group was composed of Peter, James, and John. Whenever Jesus needed to be empowered, He got together with them. They were with Him on the Mount of Transfiguration. They were with Him when He needed friendship. He called them to be with Him in His hour of deepest prayer in Gethsemane. And when they fell asleep instead of lending Him their support, He was sorely disappointed.

Some of you are thinking, "Wait a minute! He was God!" Yes, but He was God incarnated with the limitations of human flesh. All that Jesus did, He did within the same limitations that each of us experiences as human beings. He did His mighty works through prayer, and He modeled for us in His fellowship with His disciples the kind of relationship out of which spiritual power grows. Jesus never performed any miracles in His own strength. Every miracle He performed, He performed in the power of the Father who sent Him. And He demonstrated how that power can be available to each of us. He showed us that getting together in His name can provide the kind of fellowship in which His power can be experienced.

It used to be that when I strayed away from Jesus, I didn't know how to get back. I'd go to my pastor and say, "I can't pray."

My pastor would respond, "When you can't pray, pray."

That didn't make any sense to me. So I'd think, *"Maybe he's not hearing me right."*

"I can't pray," I would say again.

And he would answer, "Pray. The more you can't pray, the more you need to pray."

Today I have a good answer to the question of what to do at those times in life when I feel so devoid of the presence of God that praying seems impossible. When those times come, I depend on the three friends in my support group to get me back into a right relationship with Jesus. I don't have to depend on my own prayers to restore my empty soul. I can depend on my three friends to do that. They are responsible for me. If I am not close to Jesus, it is their fault. I have said to them, "You are responsible for where I am spiritually, even as I am responsible for each of you spiritually." We are mutually supportive. We believe that we are responsible to "bear each other's burdens" (Gal. 6:2).

Every Christian also needs a group to hold him or her

accountable for his or her behavior. Whenever my life gets messed up, my friends immediately call an emergency meeting to straighten me out. They say, "Campolo, there are certain things in your life that are screwed up, things that are contrary to the will of God, and we are here to correct you." If they didn't do that for me, I could stray away from God without even realizing I was doing so. Without their correcting ministry, I could mess up my life with ease. Each member of our group is responsible for the way the other members of the group live out their discipleship.

Do you have a support group to which you are accountable? If not, let me say this as directly as I know how: without such a small support group, you are not likely to spiritually survive.

The last thing that I want you to recognize as being essential to spiritual growth and maturity is membership in a local church. You need a church affiliation. I have to say that because so many people have become negative toward the church. Indeed, there is much to criticize about the institutional church. Pointing out the shortcomings of some local congregations is easy to do. You and I know what is wrong with the church.

I know this sounds harsh and I'm not writing it to knock anybody in particular, but these religious institutions have no right to spend $180 billion building buildings when half the world is starving to death. There is something wrong when we spend more money for stained-glass windows than we spend for feeding the hungry kids in Bangladesh. I admit that the institutional church really has its priorities messed up in a lot of other ways too. However, I still love the institutional church and I am committed to its ministry in the world. Furthermore, I believe that Jesus loves the institutional church and weeps when she fails to realize her potential.

Actually, I tried to be a pastor for a short period of my life, but I just couldn't do it right. There was a time when I was an associate pastor of a Presbyterian church in Mount Holly, New Jersey. They had two morning worship services, 8:30 and 11:00 A.M. Now, I don't know about you, but I am not wide awake in the mornings. I like to joke around and say that I am a Baptist and Baptists don't believe that God is up at 8:30 in the morning!

Anyway, I was not married at the time; I was still dating. And on Saturday nights—or should I say, Sunday mornings, I would get in much later than a man of God should. One particular Sunday morning, I staggered out of bed and went down to the church to set up for the early morning service. Back then I was responsible for the whole thing except the sermon; the senior pastor had the sermon. I managed to get everything ready and the service got under way at 8:30 A.M. One of the things for which I was responsible was the pastoral prayer.

Now in the Presbyterian church they always end the prayer with this statement: "We ask all these things in the name of the One who taught us to pray together saying, 'Our Father who art in heaven, hallowed be Thy name . . . ,'" and you know the rest. That morning, I got to the end of the pastoral prayer, and I sleepily said, "And we ask all these things in the name of the One who taught us to pray together saying," and before I could catch myself, I heard myself saying, "Now I lay me down to sleep . . ." It did not go over well at all.

The worst part of all was that it was Mother's Day. I don't know what it is like at your church, but in that church, Mother's Day is a sentimental orgy. Man, they give out flowers to everybody: to the oldest mother, to the youngest mother (usually the youngest mother is some mother who shouldn't be a mother in the first place but they give her a flower anyway), to everybody. Then they sing "Faith of Our Mothers, Living Still"—the works! It's kind of nice, but that Sunday I couldn't enjoy it because I had just blown the pastoral prayer.

Before I could recover, it was time for me to read the Scripture. I blew the Scripture too. The Scripture was 2 Timothy 1, which is about Lois and Eunice, the mother and grandmother of Timothy. Lovely passage for Mother's Day. In my haste, instead of turning to 2 Timothy, the first chapter—and you can see this one coming—I turned to 1 Timothy. To say that 1 Timothy, the first chapter, is inappropriate for Mother's Day is putting it mildly. I mean, picture all those women sitting there with these smug, Mother's Day looks on their faces and you know how mothers get on Mother's Day (it's enough to make you sick)—listening to me read the wrong passage of Scripture. I read, "And in the last days there shall be whoremongers, adulteresses, fornicators . . ." You could just feel the negative vibrations rippling all through the group. The last verse that I read ended, ". . . and murderers of mothers." It was shortly after that that I stopped being a Presbyterian and became a Baptist.

Seriously, the institutional church and Christianity deserve a closer look. Sure there are people who criticize the church. They say it is full of hypocrites. It is. That is why everyone is welcome there. The only difference between the hypocrites inside the church and the hypocrites outside the church is that the hypocrites outside the church don't *know* they are hypocrites.

Everybody is hypocritical. A hypocrite is somebody who does not consistently live out what he believes. I don't consistently live out what I believe. Every day I ask Jesus to make me more consistent with what I believe the Scriptures require me to be. But, to use biblical terminology, "It has not yet appeared what I shall be." I am still in the process of becoming the person that Jesus has molded for me.

To make my point, let's play a game of make-believe. Imagine that you are taking me on a tour of a hospital. You take me through the various wards and show me all the patients. As we come out of the hospital, suppose I say to you, "I don't like this hospital; everybody in it is sick." Undoubtedly, you would look at me in an incredulous manner and say, "Of course they are sick. Hospitals are places where sick people come."

The church of Jesus Christ may have a good number of "sick" people in it, but thank God they know where to go for help. They know where to go to find healing. Healing the spiritually sick is what church is all about. It proclaims the Word that heals. It offers hope for the troubled. It binds up the hurts of the spiritually wounded.

However, the church is much more than a spiritual hospital. It is also a community of Christians that "edifies" the saints. In other words, the church teaches and strengthens individual Christians so that each of them can be an effective servant of God in the world.

The apostle Paul teaches that in his letter to the Ephesians: "And he gave some, apostles; and some, prophets; and some, evangelists; and some, pastors and teachers; For the perfecting of the saints, for the work of the ministry, for the edifying of the body of Christ" (Eph. 4:11–12).

Some people in your church have the God-given gift of teaching the truths of the Bible. Others may have special prayer powers that bring healing to the sick. Others may have the ability to counsel people, and others may be outstanding preachers. All of these gifted people in the church are called by God to help the members of the church become mature and dynamic Christians who can effectively minister to the needs of people in the world. The Bible teaches us that all of these people have gifts, "For the perfecting of the saints, for the work of the ministry."

I don't suppose you've ever thought of yourself as a saint before. If you haven't, please let me affirm that you are indeed a saint. According to the Bible, a saint is somebody whom God sets aside to do something special in the church and for the world. That's you! God has something special that He wants you to do for Him. That makes you a saint. If I were you, I wouldn't use the title publicly. I don't think it would go over too big. Nevertheless, it's true. You are called by God to be a saint. So are the other Christians in your church.

The Lord has prepared certain leaders in the church to teach in order to edify the saints by teaching them the Scriptures, to encourage them in spiritual ways, and to strengthen them so that they can effectively minister to the world. If the world is going to be reached for Christ, it will be reached through the saints. That's you and me. The people in your school are not coming to church. The people in your neighborhood are not coming to church. The people at the place where you work are not coming to church. You and I must go to them with the gospel.

The Bible never suggested that they would *come* to the church. Instead, the Bible instructs the church to go to the world.

The Bible orders the saints to go into the world and meet people where they live and work and play. We are supposed to tell the people of the world about Jesus as we meet them in the normal course of our daily lives. Jesus commanded us, "Go into all the world and preach the gospel." One of the primary purposes of the church is to train and strengthen the saints to do just that. Each of us needs the "edification" of the church if we are to carry out the Great Commission of Jesus.

You have a responsibility to build up your church and help it to be and do what Jesus created it to be and do. You could do so much for your church if you would just give yourself and your church a chance. For instance, if your church has a weekly prayer meeting, you could get all of your church friends together and show up. It would be wild if you didn't tell your pastor in advance. You would blow his mind. Have you ever thought of doing that? Or, have you thought of going to a church business meeting to share your beliefs and convictions about how the church can minister to the world? Your church needs your input. If you come in a loving and humble manner, the faithful workers in the church will be thrilled to see you taking an active part in the life of the church. You will be a source of encouragement to everyone.

You need the church and the church desperately needs you. If you are not affiliated with the church, you have denied yourself one of the major means through which God wants to keep you faithful to Him. You are separated from the body of Christ that seeks to prepare you to serve the world.

Okay, let's review! (1) Read the Bible. (2) Pray. (3) Start a little support group. Beyond that, be a part of a church and try to make that church into a powerful instrument to equip the saints to do the work of the ministry in the world.

People, this world has to be changed for Jesus. *We've* got to change things, and we can do it. We can end poverty for a lot of people. We can end racism in a lot of places. We can bring economic relief and social justice where they are needed. We can lead people to Jesus Christ so that they might become new creatures in Him. We can become people who are strong enough to alter history.

There is enough potential in your home church right now to significantly alter the life of your community and possibly the course of human history. However, if such things are to happen, we've got to make the church into the kind of church that God wants it to be. He does want to change this world, and He is expecting you to build His church so that His will might be done on earth as it is in heaven.

You say that the world can't be changed. It is too big, too demonic; it can't be changed or challenged. You're wrong. You and I can do it together. Together with Christ we can build a church that is such a powerful instrument of God that the gates of hell shall not prevail against it.

I belong to a black church in West Philadelphia. I've been a member of that church for decades and for me Mount Carmel Baptist Church is the closest thing to heaven this side of the pearly gates. I preach to a lot of congregations, but I have to say that no other group of people leaves me with excitement like the congregation of my home church. People in my congregation always let me know how I'm doing. Whether I am good or bad, they let me know what they are feeling about my message.

One time when I was preaching, I sensed that nothing was happening. There seemed to be no movement of the dynamism of God. I was struggling, as you have seen ministers struggle, and seemed to be getting nowhere. I had gotten about three-quarters of the way through my sermon when some lady on the back row yelled, "Help him, Jesus! Help him, Jesus!" That was all the evidence I needed that things were not going well that day.

On the other hand, when the preacher is really "on" in my church, they let him know. The deacons sit right under the pulpit, and whenever the preacher says something especially good, they cheer him on by yelling, "Preach, brother! Preach, brother! Preach, man, preach!" And I want to tell you that when they do that to me, it makes me want to preach.

The women in my church have a special way of responding when the preacher is "doing good." They usually wave one hand in the air and call out to the preacher, "Well. Well." Whenever they do that to me, my hormones bubble.

But that's not all. When I really get going, the men in my congregation shout encouragement by saying, "Keep going, brother! Keep going! Keep going!" I assure you that a preacher never gets that kind of reaction from a white congregation. White people never yell, "Keep going! Keep going!" White audiences are more likely to check their watches and mumble, "Stop! Stop!"

One Good Friday there were seven of us preaching back to back, each of us trying to outdo the others. When it was my turn to preach, I rolled into high gear and I want to tell you, I was good. The more I preached, the more the people in that congregation "turned on," and the more they "turned on," the better I got. I got better and better and better. I got so good that I wanted to take notes on me! At the end of my message, the congregation broke loose. I was absolutely thrilled to hear the hallelujahs and the cries of joy that broke loose throughout the place. I sat down next to my pastor and he looked at me with a smile. He reached down with his hand and squeezed my knee. "You did all right, boy!" he said. (I must admit that I hate it when he calls me "boy!")

I turned to him and asked, "Pastor, are you going to be able to top that?"

The old man smiled at me and he said, "Son, you just sit back, 'cause this old man is going to do you in!"

I didn't figure that anybody could surpass me that day. I

had been so good. . . . But the old guy got up, and I have to admit, he did me in. The amazing thing was that he did it with the use of one line. That line was "It's Friday, but Sunday's comin'!" That statement may not blow you away, but you should have heard him do it. He started his sermon real softly by saying, "It was Friday. It was Friday, and my Jesus was dead on the tree. But that was Friday, and Sunday's comin'!"

One of the deacons yelled, "Preach, brother! Preach!" It was all the encouragement that he needed. He came on louder as he said, "It was Friday, and Mary was cryin' her eyes out. The disciples were runnin' in every direction like sheep without a shepherd, but that was Friday and Sunday's comin'!" People in the congregation were beginning to pick up the message. Women were waving their hands and calling softly, "Well, well." Some of the men were yelling, "Keep going! Keep going!"

The preacher kept going. He picked up the volume still more and shouted, "It was Friday. The cynics were lookin' at the world and sayin', 'As things have been so they shall be. You can't change anything in this world, you can't change anything.' But those cynics didn't know that it was only Friday. Sunday's comin'!

"It was Friday! And on Friday, those forces that oppress the poor and make the poor to suffer were in control. But that was Friday! Sunday's comin'!

"It was Friday, and on Friday Pilate thought he had washed his hands of a lot of trouble. The Pharisees were struttin' around, laughin' and pokin' each other in the ribs. They thought they were back in charge of things, but they didn't know that it was only Friday! Sunday's comin'!"

He kept on working that one phrase for a half-hour, then an hour, then an hour and a quarter, then an hour and a half. Over and over he came at us, "It's Friday, but Sunday's comin'! It's Friday, but Sunday's comin'! It's Friday, but Sunday's comin'!"

By the time he had come to the end of the message, I was exhausted. He had me and everybody else so worked up that I don't think any of us could have stood it much longer. At the end of his message he just yelled at the top of his lungs, "IT'S FRIDAY!" and all five hundred of us in that church yelled back with one accord, "SUNDAY'S COMIN'!"

Always remember that. Remember that Sunday is coming. Get into the Word, pray, form a support group, build up the church, make the church an instrument that will change the world. And though it often seems so dark and dismal, we have the good news, and the good news is this: though the world is dark and dismal and demonic, we are going to challenge it, we are going to resist it, we are going to transform it by the grace of God and we will be here to declare the good news. And the good news is this: it is Friday, but Sunday's coming!